THE KNIGHTS TEMPLAR AND SCOTLAND

THE KNIGHTS TEMPLAR AND SCOTLAND

ROBERT FERGUSON

Dedicated to Peggy,
and to Shari and Tim

First published 2010

The History Press
The Mill, Brimscombe Port
Stroud, Gloucestershire, GL5 2QG
www.thehistorypress.co.uk

British Library Cataloguing in Publication Data.
A catalogue record for this book is available from the British Library.

ISBN 978 0 7524 5183 1

Typesetting and origination by The History Press
Printed in India by Aegean Offset Printers, New Delhi

CONTENTS

Illustrations		6
Acknowledgements		8
Preface		10
1	The Knights Templar of Jerusalem	15
2	Balantrodoch: The Life of the Templars	46
3	Templar Life, Rights and Privileges	60
4	The Excommunication of Robert the Bruce	76
5	The Templars' Arrests	83
6	The Templars' Flight to Scotland	93
7	Scotland's Templar Inquisition	107
8	The Knights Templar and the Battle of Bannockburn	115
9	Rosslyn Chapel: A Templar Legacy?	129
10	The Templars after Bannockburn	140
11	The Modern Scottish Knights Templar	154
Appendix: Could there have been Templars at Bannockburn?		169
Bibliography		177
Index		183
About the Author		192

ILLUSTRATIONS

1. St Bernard, Abbot of Clairvaux (1090–1153). Fifteenth-century illumination by Jean Fauquet from the Hours of Etienne Chevalier. (Musée Conde, Chantilly, France/Giraudon/Bridgeman Art Library)
2. The Burning of the Templars, *c.* 1308. Fourteenth-century engraving by French School. (British Library, London, UK, Bridgeman Art Library)
3. Jacques de Molay, *c.* 1243–1314. (Bridgeman Art Library, Getty Images)
4. The Old Temple Church at Temple. (Crown Copyright: Royal Commission on the Ancient and Historical Monuments of Scotland)
5. Castle Sween. (© 2008, Robert Ferguson)
6. Grave slab at Kilmartin in display house. (© 2008, Robert Ferguson)
7. Kilmartin Church. (© 2008, Robert Ferguson)
8. Grave slab at Kilmartin in the cemetery. (© 2008, Robert Ferguson)
9. Kilmory Church. (© 2008, Robert Ferguson)
10. Statue of Robert the Bruce. (Photographed by John Boak, National Trust for Scotland)
11. Bruce's forensic reconstructed head. (Photographed by Allan Forbes, National Trust for Scotland)
12. Map of options for locations for day two of the Battle of Bannockburn. (*The Battle of Bannockburn*, a Report for Stirling Council, by Fiona Watson, Ph.D. and Maggie Anderson, Ph.D.)

13. Rosslyn Chapel. (© Antonia Reeve/Rosslyn Chapel Trust)
14. General inside view. Looking east towards the main alter. (© Antonia Reeve/Rosslyn Chapel Trust)
15. Sinclair burial stone. (© Antonia Reeve/Rosslyn Chapel Trust)
16. Knight on Horseback. (© Antonia Reeve/Rosslyn Chapel Trust)
17. Green Man. (© Antonia Reeve/Rosslyn Chapel Trust)

ACKNOWLEDGEMENTS

First I would like to thank the staff at the National Archives of Scotland and the National Library of Scotland. For an American who was foraging around looking for ancient documents and old books, their help was invaluable.

J. Connall Bell and Patricia Tennyson Bell are to be thanked for providing me with the motivation to begin writing this book. Along this line, special thanks go to John Flemming, a Scot whose opinion about the Templars being at Bannockburn was, and is, unequivocal.

In Scotland, special thanks go to Stuart Morris of Balgonie for providing a link between the past and the present. I cannot thank George Stewart enough for putting the current Scottish Templar Orders in perspective. Ron Sinclair and Bill Hunter provided me with their generous help in connecting me with sources of information about the current Templar community and about Alexander Deuchar. Also, thanks go to John Ritchie who provided me with an initial connection with the *Milit Templi Scotia*.

On the practical side, I would like to thank Victoria Kibler who proofed and edited my manuscript. Thanks also go to Jonathon Kibler-McCabe, who speaks fluent Gaelic, and to Bronwyn Jones who translated works originally in French that went back to the eighteenth century. The Appendix could not have been written without the help of Don Bentley, a Professor Emeritus, Pomona College, who specialises in statistics.

The help of Simon Hamlet of The History Press in guiding me through the initial process was invaluable, as was that of Robin Harries. Special thanks go to Abigail Wood, my editor, who converted the language of a lawyer and the format of a legal brief to a very readable book. And, finally, there is my wife Peggy, who put up with me when I was cloistered in the study, and who motivated me when I needed encouragement to continue.

PREFACE

At the bottom of the letterhead stationary for the *Ordo Supremus Militaris Templi Hierosolymitani*, Grand Priory of the Scots, is the phrase:

Scotland – The Unbroken Templar Link.

This book had its beginning when I asked the Grand Bailiff if that phrase was true, and where could I find the information to back it up? His answer was yes, the statement was true, but no, he did not know exactly where the information could be found. This prompted my naive reply, 'I'll find out', thinking the answer was simple and that it could be the subject for an article in the Priory's newsletter.

What started as a simple question turned into a major project that has required over three years of research and writing. It quickly became apparent that over the last hundred years, little has been written about the Knights Templar in Scotland. This was particularly true for the period from 1314, the year of the Battle of Bannockburn, to the early 1960s. During this period, there were various antidotal references and a lot of speculation, but I could find no easily referenced historical facts. This raised the question, if a substantial amount of effort is going to be required to answer my first question, why not write a book?

Another reason for this book is a statement from my good friend John Fleming, a Scot who now lives in southern California, but still returns to Scotland for a couple of months each summer. When I mentioned I was writing a book about the Templars and Scotland, he replied, 'Oh, you mean at Bannockburn.'

I was surprised and asked, 'What do you mean? Do you know about them?'

'Of course,' he answered. 'Everybody does.'

'But how?' I asked. 'Nothing has been written.'

'It's just passed down,' he said. 'Everyone knows the Templars were at Bannockburn. You hear about it.'

In line with John's statement, I thought the best place to begin the quest was with the oft-asked question, were the Knights Templar present at the Battle of Bannockburn? But the Battle of Bannockburn happened two years after the formal dissolution of the Templars, and seven years after King Philip IV of France issued the warrants for their arrest on 13 October 1307. From this, it became clear that before Bannockburn could be analyzed, it was necessary to research the history of the Knights Templar in Scotland from the time of their arrival in 1127, until their arrest and dissolution. But an understanding of Scotland's Templar history required a good general knowledge of who and what the Templars were. There were no Templar battles in Scotland. In Scotland the Templars were monks, recruiters, landlords and businessmen. So, in order to insure that all the readers have a basic knowledge of the Templars, the book begins by describing these aspects of Templar life, followed by their battles and activities in Palestine.

Most of what is written concerning the Knights Templar in Scotland consists of articles written in the late nineteenth and early twentieth centuries. I found that these tend to be anecdotal, concentrate on the detail of particular events, and do not provide a description that leads to an understanding of the lives of the medieval Knights Templar. After several readings of the available materials, it became apparent that the information about who and what the Templars were in Scotland revolved around their headquarters, Balantrodoch, and the management of their hundreds of properties that existed throughout Scotland.

Why did the Templars come to Scotland? The answer to this question lies, to a great extent, in the excommunication in 1304 of the Scottish king, Robert the Bruce. This event is significant not only in explaining the flight of the Knights Templar to Scotland, but in explaining their reasons for staying there. Clement V was Pope when the French King Philip IV ordered their arrest, and it was Clement V who formally dissolved the Knights Templar. As significant as this event is, there is little modern discussion of it. Most historians give it no more than a few sentences. While the reason for the excommunication may be well known, I could not find a consistent version of the events leading up to it. In Chapter 4 I outline a number of the various versions.

Until the Battle of Bannockburn, most of what occurred in Scotland is tied to what happened first in Europe. In order that the reader might understand the Templars' flight to Scotland, I recount the events that led to the Templars' arrest in Chapter 5.

There has been much speculation on the question of whether the Templars actually fled from France prior to their arrests, and whether they went to Scotland. While there is no direct evidence that they did, the circumstantial evidence is overwhelming. It begins with the recently disclosed fact that the Templars' second in command, Hugh de Pairaud, knew of the coming arrests and told his brothers. Then, not only were the Templars safe in Scotland, but Scotland provided a place where they could continue living as both monks and warriors. I have divided this subject into two parts. Chapter 6 describes the Templars' flight, and the Appendix analyzes whether a sufficient number of qualified Templars would have been available to assist Robert the Bruce at Bannockburn.

In France, the Templars were subject to trial by King Philip IV, and an inquisition by Pope Clement V. They were threatened with, and in some cases suffered, unspeakable torture. This applied to not only the knights, but also to the hundreds of sergeants and others involved with the Order. In Scotland there were arrests, and there was an inquisition, of sorts. But as I describe in Chapter 7, it primarily involved the Templars' attitude and ended up being much ado about nothing.

Were the Templars present at the Battle of Bannockburn? Most Knights Templar who are Scots, or are of Scottish ancestry, believe, like my friend John Fleming, that without question the answer is 'yes'. The belief for many is absolute. But is it historically provable? Is there any unequivocal, historical evidence to back up the belief? The answer is that there is little or none. But as to whether or not there is circumstantial evidence that is more than speculation, the answer is yes, there is. Chapter 8 describes the events leading up to the Battle of Bannockburn, and the probable presence of the Knights Templar. When I viewed the events and circumstances leading up to the battle, I developed an entirely new theory about the Templars' role in it.

Rosslyn Chapel has been described as being closely associated with the Knights Templar. Was it? Or was it simply an extraordinary collegiate chapel that was used by the Saint Clair (Sinclair) family for worship and burials? Is the symbolism tied to the Templar myths and mysticism? Or is it simply representative of the time? In Chapter 9, 'Rosslyn Chapel: a Templar Legacy?' I discuss these and other points.

This brings up the initial question, is there an unbroken Templar link in Scotland? What happened to the Knights Templar after the Battle of Bannockburn? After their formal dissolution, how were the Templars in Scotland involved with the Knights of Saint John of Jerusalem (the Hospitallers)? Were there periods when the Templars went into decline? Did they disappear to the outside world? The answers do not appear to be a part of what we accept as recorded history. After three years of research, the answers to these and several other questions begin to come together in Chapter 10. Also, there may be secret histories in the files of the Templar Orders in Scotland that are considered too controversial for release. Or they may simply be inconsistent with known facts and recorded history. I do not know all the answers, but Chapter 10 contains some of them. It and Chapter 8 are written with the hope that they open avenues for further exploration and disclosure.

Chapter 11, 'The Modern Scottish Knights Templar', is an overview of today's Templar Orders in Scotland. Thanks to the internet, anyone can go online and look up the websites for most of the modern Templar organizations. But I have found that a background and history exists for a number of the modern international and Scottish Orders that is not online. In terms of Scotland, the Templars are in the midst of a strong revival.

1

THE KNIGHTS TEMPLAR OF JERUSALEM

Who were the Knights Templar? What were they? These questions are particularly important in the context of Scotland because in Scotland their purpose was purely economic, and their only engagements were Bannockburn and the battles that led up to it. But still, in Scotland the Templars had a purpose, and no less a mystique than the mystique that existed in France and Palestine. To that end, this chapter describes who the Templars were and what they did. It is not meant to be exhaustive. For this, there are several books listed in the Bibliography.

If the Templars fled to Scotland after their arrest in France, would they have been inclined to stay there? The answer to this question is found in the description of how the Templars lived, and what aspects of their life-style in Europe and Palestine were consistent with their life in Scotland. There is also the question of whether the Templars were present at the Battle of Bannockburn. Would the Templars have remained in a fighting mode for eight years?

The Knights Templar are often described as 'warrior-monks'. Most authors emphasize the Templars' battles, with some discussion of their extensive commercial and banking activities. But there is little discussion about a Templar Knight's daily life, or how he lived as a monk. Because Scotland involved no Templar battles, and was exclusively a commercial center devoted to raising money, a more complete picture of the Templars is essential.

The Order began as the Order of the Poor Knights of Christ and the Temple of Solomon, and ultimately became the *Ordo Supremus Militaris Templi Hierosolymitane*, the Sovereign Military Order of the Temple of Jerusalem, or the Knights Templar. It was formed in 1119 by Hughes de Payens and Godfrey of Saint Omer to defend Christian pilgrims in the Holy Land during their pilgrimages to Jerusalem.[1] The Order was made up of knights and other nobles who took the vows of a monk. It became the world's most effective fighting force and first multinational conglomerate.

The Order was formed as a result of the First Crusade that ended in 1099 with the capture of Palestine (known to Europeans as 'Outremer', the land beyond the sea) and the city of Jerusalem. With the capture of Jerusalem came a flood of pilgrims from Europe to visit the Holy Land. There were an immense number of pilgrims and their need for protection was the catalyst for the formation of the Knights Templar.

The Templars' primary founder, Hughes de Payens, was a knight who came from the village of Payens in the province of Champagne on the left bank of the River Seine in northern France. He was a vassal of, and owed his allegiance to, Hugh, the Count de Champagne. The Templars originally consisted of nine knights: Hughes de Payens, Godfroi de St Omer, Roral, Gundemar, Godfrey Bisol, Payens de Montidier, Archambaud de St Aman, Andrew de Monthar and the Count of Provence.[2] The number of knights remained essentially the same for nine years. The only known change was the addition of Hugh, Count de Champagne, in 1226. He was a powerful noble who brought a great deal of credibility to the early Templars. The Templars' purpose was to assist and protect the pilgrims as they traveled from Mediterranean ports, usually Jaffa or Tyre, to Jerusalem, and from there to the other holy places in Palestine. This need existed because the Christians held the cities and holy places, but could not control the routes in between. As a result, the routes were constantly under threat by marauders, thieves and the people who had been dispossessed of their homes as a result of the First Crusade.

Housing for the original knights was unusual. Initially they had none. But at Hughes de Payens' request, Baldwin I of Jerusalem permitted the Templars to live in a wing of his palace over the catacombs of the former Temple of Solomon. It is not known how the original nine Templars, who lived in poverty and relied on handouts for food and clothing, were able to protect travelers and stay alive in Outremer for nine years. First, disease was a significant problem for Europeans who traveled to Palestine. Then there is the question of how only nine knights could protect thousands of pilgrims and themselves, and stay alive against the Arabs who continued to fight as bands of mounted armed outlaws.

It is believed by many that the Templars' primary purpose during the first nine years was excavation in the catacombs beneath the ruins of the Temple of Solomon.[3] What was found is a matter of great discussion, debate and dispute. There are various suppositions. They range from the Holy Grail, to the Ark of the Covenant, to an immense amount of precious metals and jewels, to the scrolls of Jesus' brother James the Just, to evidence of a marriage between Jesus of Nazareth and Mary Magdalene,[4] to nothing at all. Some of the theories do appear to have a historical basis. Early in Templar history (apparently within the first nine years), Hughes de Payens is said to have written that 'although Christendom seemed to have forgotten them [the Templars], God had not, and the fact that their work was in secret would win them a greater reward from God.'[5] But there is no evidence that indicates why the Templars' work was in secret, or what their work was.

The evidence that does exist simply confirms that the Templars explored the catacombs under the Temple of Solomon. In the latter part of the nineteenth century Lieutenant Charles Warren of the Royal Engineers was part of a team that conducted an excavation of the catacombs. Among a number of discoveries, Lieutenant Warren found a variety of Templar artifacts, including a spur, the remains of a lance, a small Templar cross and the major part of a Templar sword. These artifacts are now in Scotland and are part of a private collection owned by Robert Brydon, a Templar historian and archivist.

Much has been written about the Templars' battles, their victories, and defeats. Likewise, much was also written about their downfall, the charges that were ultimately brought against the Templars in 1307, and their trials for heresy.[6] But little has been written about just who they were, how they lived, their organization, or whether they continued to exist in Scotland after they were officially suppressed and disbanded in 1312 by Pope Clement V. The Templars lived a life that conditioned them to be organized and devout. Their duties involved not only fighting in battles, but living an austere life that focused on the preservation of their Order, their traditions and their property.

To understand the Templars one must first look at what knights generally were, and what they were not. In the Middle Ages, knights were not looked upon favorably. As succinctly put by Peter Partner in *The Knights Templar and their Myth*:

> Far from idealizing chivalry, religious leaders usually represented knightly life as lawless, licentious, and bloody. The Clergy were absolutely forbidden to shed blood, and to combine the life of an active soldier, killing and plundering like any other soldier, with the life of a monk, was to go against a fundamental principle.[7]

But this description did not apply to the Templars. The Templars' mentor, Abbot Bernard de Clairvaux, who ultimately became Saint Bernard, and who is depicted in a fifteenth-century painting shown in Figure 1, was strident in his belief in the Templars, and was eloquent in his expression. This is illustrated in his essay 'In Praise of the New Knighthood', which he wrote in the early 1130s to Hughes de Payens. In modern terminology, it was a masterful sales tool for recruiting knights, and soliciting support and gifts. The following quotes are examples:

> The new order of knights is one that is unknown by the ages. They fight two wars, one against adversaries of flesh and blood, and another against a spiritual army of wickedness in the heavens.
> [...]
> Truly, his is a fearless knight and completely secure. While his body is properly armed for these circumstances, his soul is also clothed with the armour of faith. On all sides surely his is well armed; he fears neither demons nor men. Truly does he not fear death, but instead he longs for death. Why should he have a fear for life or for death, when in Christ is to live, and to die is to gain? He stands faithfully and with confidence in the service of Christ; he greatly desires for release and to be with Christ, the latter certainly a more gracious thing.
> [...]
> Even more amazing is that they can be gentle like a lamb, or ferocious like a lion. I do not know whether I should address them as monks or as knights, perhaps they should be recognised as both. But as monks they have gentleness, and as knights military fortitude.[8]

As the Order evolved, the Templars were ultimately governed by a detailed set of regulations, appropriately named the 'Rule'. What caused the Rule to be written is a matter of dispute. According to Malcolm Barber, the guiding hand was Saint Bernard, but the actual wording of the Rule was a 'fairly exhaustive process of committee discussion'.[9] This view is disputed by Lynn Picket and Clive Prince who contend that 'Bernard actually wrote the Templars' Rule – which was based on that of the Cistercians ...'[10]

Regardless of how the Rule was written, it absolutely controlled the life of a Templar Knight, whether he was fighting in the east or involved in commerce in the west. Under the Rule, a Templar's lifestyle was beyond austere. He lived as a monk who cropped his hair, let his beard grow and, to avoid temptations of the flesh and to be ready when needed, he always slept clothed.[11] The Templar Knight ate meat only three times a week.[12] He spent a great deal of his time in silence.[13] There was no gossip or small talk.[14] The knight lived in a dormitory-like building and was allowed no privacy. He could not use or own locks. If he received a letter it had to be read to him out loud in the presence of the Master[15] or possibly a chaplain.

While the Templars did not have the powers and sanctity of the priesthood, each day when he was not in battle, which was most of the time, he performed the six liturgical prayers. This occurred every day of a knight's life. The normal Templar's day began early at 4 a.m. with the day's first liturgical prayer, Matins. The Templar brothers would recite thirteen Paternosters (Lord's Prayers) and prayers to Our Lady. They would then tend to their horses and equipment. This was followed by Prime at 6 a.m. which included more prayers and Mass. Then at 11.30 came Sext and the reciting of additional Paternosters and prayers to Our Lady.

After Sext came the afternoon meal, which was eaten in silence. At 2.30 came Nones and more prayers. Then Vespers at 6 p.m. was followed by the evening meal. The sixth and final liturgical prayer was sung at Compline, after which the Templar Knight would attend to his horses and then retire.[16]

In between the times for prayer and meals, the primary tasks for the Templar Knight in Outremer were tending to his horses and arms, and keeping ready for battle. Each knight also worked in the fields and filled in where needed with other simple tasks. The Templars were not permitted to, and never did, remain idle. This routine was followed day in and day out. It did not vary. It applied to all Templars, including knights and sergeants, and all those who abandoned secular life and chose the communal life of the Templars.[17] Once one became accustomed to the routine it became part of the Templar's life, whether he be a knight, sergeant, chaplain or a committed menial worker. The routine was followed in Outremer and in all parts of Europe and the British Isles. The level of commitment is demonstrated by the amount of torture that the French king had to exert, or threaten, before he could begin to extract confessions after the knights' arrests.

On the battlefield the Knights Templar were not only superlative horsemen who constantly trained to perfect tight formations, but were fearless, and dedicated to victory over the Saracens. To this end, they were not permitted to retreat unless the odds against them were at least three to one. In some cases the Templars did not retreat until their forces were outnumbered six to one. Even then, they could not leave the field unless ordered to do so. Surrender was useless because the Templars could not use their funds for ransom. As a result, Templars taken in battle were either traded or, more often, summarily executed.[18] After 1229, when the Templars became an organized fighting force, with up to four horses per knight, a squire and excellent armament, the average lifespan of a Templar Knight who chose to remain in Outremer was about five years.

Even before the adoption of the Rule, each Templar Knight took vows of absolute poverty, chastity and obedience before Warmund of Picquigny, Patriarch of Jerusalem.[19] Surprisingly, only two of the three vows were incorporated into the Rule. Poverty was assumed. The applicable Rules and practices were severe:

Chastity was a very important vow. In the charges brought by King Philip IV of France, sexual deviancy was almost a theme. Yet the writers and commentators are uniform in their opinion that there was little if any lewd or untoward conduct among the Templars. What faults there were lay in the areas of secrecy and avarice which is discussed in later chapters. Chastity was codified in the Rule, article 71, which states:

> We believe it to be a dangerous thing for any religious to look too much upon the face of woman. For this reason none of you may presume to kiss a woman, be it widow, young girl, mother, sister, aunt or any other; and henceforth the Knighthood of Jesus Christ should avoid at all cost

the embraces of women, by which men have perished many times, so that they may remain eternally before the face of God with a pure conscience and sure life.

Obedience was absolute. It was codified in the Rule at article 39, which states that:

For nothing is dearer to Jesus Christ than obedience. For as soon as something is commanded by the Master or by him to whom the master has given the authority, it should be done without delay as though Christ himself had commanded it.

While there is no specific article in the Rule which commands poverty, the specifics of how a Templar Knight lived left no alternative. Poverty is recognized in the Rule at article 58, which deals with tithes which could be received on behalf of the Order. It states:

You now have abandoned the pleasant riches of this world, we believe you to have willingly subjected yourselves to poverty; therefore we are resolved that you who live the communal life may receive tithes.

Even though the Templar brothers in Scotland were involved only in real estate, commerce and money markets, the Templar Knights lived by the Rule and it was strictly enforced.[20]

THE TEMPLAR HIERARCHY

Every large organization has its bureaucracy. This was as true in the Middle Ages as it is today and the Order was no exception. The Templars not only had a bureaucratic hierarchy, it had specific job descriptions. These primarily evolved between 1129–1160 when the Templars established what today would be called an organization chart or its organizational 'hierarchy'. The hierarchy demonstrates that some things never change. Not even in 800 years. The Templars' organization chart looks just like many seen today.

The Templars' organizational hierarchy was used, to some extent, in Scotland. Some of the offices were the same, others were unique to Scotland. But an understanding of how the Templar organization worked in general, provides a basis for understanding how it was adjusted to accommodate the conditions in Scotland.

The organizational hierarchy was logically codified in the portion of the Rule known as the Hierarchical Statutes. Each of the offices is described separately and listed in sequence, the higher offices first.

Grand Master: The Master of the Temple of Jerusalem was the ultimate leader of the Knights Templar. Although his powers were extensive and his authority in battle absolute, the Rule expressly required that the major internal decisions had to be approved by a Council of Knights, of which the Master was a member, with one vote.[21]

Seneschal: The Seneschal was second in command to the Grand Master and had the Grand Master's full authority in his absence. As the Grand Master's 'right-hand man' he carried the beauseant or piebald, the Templars' black and white banner with the white above and the black below.[22]

Marshal: The Marshal was third in command. He was in charge of all arms and animals used in battle. He was also responsible for the distribution of gifts, alms and booty. In the absence of the Master and the Seneschal, the Marshal was the supreme military commander.[23]

Commander (Grand Marshal/Prior) of the Kingdom of Jerusalem/ Grand Treasurer: He was the commander for the province of Jerusalem and was the treasurer for the entire Order.[24]

Commander (Master) of the City of Jerusalem: He ran the city and continued the original task of the Knights Templar: protecting pilgrims en route to Jerusalem. There was a Master for each country who ruled over the commanderies and preceptories in each respective country, such as France, Germany, Italy, Spain and England. The Templars in Scotland were ruled by the Commander or Preceptor at Balantrodoch who reported to the Master in London.[25]

Draper: The Draper was the quartermaster. He was in charge of clothes and bed linen.[26]

Turcopolier: The Turcopolier was the light cavalry commander who developed several battle formations. As described in Chapter 10, one of these is said to have been used by Scottish knights in Spain against the Moors when they were attempting to take the heart of Robert the Bruce to Outremer.

The Rule describes the commanders and sergeants who were responsible for the localized units, specifically the local properties of the Templars, forts, farms, and estates which were called 'houses'. These were governed by Commanders of the Houses who reported to the Provincial Master or Grand Prior. England and Scotland were not separated and were governed by a Master of the Temple in London. Scotland was governed by a Commander or Preceptor at Balantrodoch just south of Edinburgh, which is described in detail in the next chapter.

Specific levels or classes in the Templar brothers existed. For example:

A **knight** was noble before he joined the Order. He did not become a knight by joining. Upon joining the Order he surrendered his property, if he had any, took monastic vows and became a monk. He wore a white mantle with a red eight-pointed cross.[27]

An **associate** was a noble who joined the Order for limited periods of time or a fixed term.[28] For example, a married man would become involved for a while. Another might join the Order for a particular crusade. After his term was up, he would return home to his family and estate.

A **sergeant** (or **esquire**) was a younger, lightly armed troop and/or a squire to a knight. He was required to be a free man to be qualified to join. He wore the red eight-pointed cross on a brown or black mantle. He was not allowed to wear a white mantle.[29] At the inquisition of the Templars in Scotland, only two knights were questioned; the majority of the brothers in Scotland were undoubtedly sergeants whose job it was to conduct the overall management of the Templar properties. None were arrested, and the records show that they simply went on as before.

A Templar **chaplain** replaced and was separate from the church or diocesan authority. The chaplain conducted all of the Templars' various religious services and ceremonies. He answered only to the Pope.[30]

Craftsmen and **menials** were the manual laborers, artisans and domestic servants who are said to have been the largest group of Templar personnel. They performed the day-to-day work.[31] The elite of this group were the stonemasons.

In Scotland the most numerous group were the **baillis** who may have played a significant role in the Templars' continued existence in Scotland after their formal dissolution. An individual baillis would manage a larger estate or house. Others would manage a number of smaller properties. None were arrested during the inquisition in Scotland. They and their successors continued to manage the Templar properties in Scotland for several hundred years.

WARRIORS AND ENTREPRENEURS

The Templars' roles as warriors and entrepreneurs began in 1229 after the Council of Troyes. In late 1227 or early 1228 Hughes de Payens left Palestine and returned to France, where he began an earnest campaign to solicit gifts and gain recruits. He met with the kings and nobility of France, and then traveled to Normandy where he met with Henry I, the King of England, who gave him 'his blessing and great treasures'. Henry I then sent him off to raise funds and to recruit additional knights from England and Scotland.[32] Before and at the Council of Troyes, Hughes de Payens had a long dialogue with Abbot Bernard de Clairvaux, which ended with the Abbot's full support. As a result, the Templars established a strong foothold in France, England and Scotland.[33] Ultimately, the Templars acquired land in Outremer, Italy, Spain, Portugal, Ireland and Germany. 'If the brothers in the Holy Land were the spearhead, those in Europe were the shaft, supplying arms and armor, men, money, horses and food.'[34]

The Templars ultimately formed the predecessor to what is today's multinational conglomerate.[35] They owned churches, forts, farms and extensive landholdings throughout Europe and Outremer. They became very skilled in farming, particularly on barely profitable land, because nobles often donated land that was not economical for them to farm themselves. Another area in which the Templars excelled was stonemasonry; there was a specific rule that expressly permitted masons to wear gloves, when all the other brothers, except chaplains, could not.[36]

The Templars also owned a substantial fleet of ships. Because of their military ability and reputation, they were able to safely move goods and money. They controlled the Atlantic coast from their port at La Rochelle, the Mediterranean from Marseilles, and the east from Acre in Outremer. They were multinational bankers who held money and

wealth on deposit for monarchs and nobles, and also loaned them substantial amounts. The Knights Templar invented the letter of credit. These
originated with travelers depositing money in London or Paris, and then
drawing the equivalent in a different currency at their destination in the
east. This, of course, generated a fee. The practice was quickly incorporated into the practices of secular bankers. While the Church prohibited
the charging of interest, the Templars and other bankers could charge
fees and levy penalties.

Another area where the Templars were self-contained was in
healthcare.[37] The Rule is very specific about providing care and consid-
eration to brothers who became sick.[38] They had their own hospitals,[39]
physicians and surgeons. The Templars could provide excellent healthcare because they had become intimately familiar with near eastern
medicine which was substantially superior to the primitive methods
used in Europe. They are even believed to have had an understanding
of antibiotics.[40] If a Templar contracted leprosy, which was not un-
common, he was given the option of transferring to the Order of St
Lazarus.[41]

It is more exciting to write about the Templars' battles, and to depict
the Templars primarily as warriors. But warriors spend a great deal of
time in between battles, and the knights of the Knights Templar were
no exception. They spent the majority of their time performing maintenance on their weapons, caring for their livestock, tending to their
agriculture and banking. On a daily basis, the knights were monks and
they lived communally. Each was provided according to his need. No
one knight was elevated above another.[42] They not only said grace at
each meal,[43] but they read from the Holy Scripture.[44] They celebrated
nineteen feast days.[45] They had specific rules for attendance at chapel,[46]
and on Fridays the knights ate only Lenten food, which was eaten
collectively.[47] In the evening, each day ended with prayers.[48] And so
it went, every day for approximately 183 years between the Council
of Troyes in 1129 and the Templars' formal dissolution in 1312, from
England and Scotland, across Europe to Outremer. This represents a
significant amount of structure and tradition. To attempt to end the
Templars' long conditioned lifestyle on a particular day, such as the day
of the Templar arrests on Friday 13 October 1307, or with the stroke of
a pen by Pope Clement V on 3 April 1312 when he signed the decree
dissolving the Templars, would be next to impossible.

THE HISTORY OF THE KNIGHTS TEMPLAR

The Templars may have originated in 1118, when Hughes de Payens and eight other knights began protecting pilgrims traveling in the Holy Land, but their chronicled history begins in 1128 after the Council of Troyes. It was then that the Templars began their defence of the Holy Land, and they led its occupation for 162 years.

The Council of Troyes took place in the cathedral at Troyes on 13 January 1128, St Hilary's day. It is near to both the towns of Payens (now 'Payns') and Clairvaux in northern France. We know exactly what happened at the council because the proceedings were recorded by John Michael, who Bernard de Clairvaux chose to be the council's scribe. The council was presided over by Matthew du Remois, Cardinal-Bishop of Albano, the papal legate. Hughes de Payens was accompanied by the Templars' co-founder, Godfrey de Saint-Omar, and four other original Templars, Roland Geoffroi Bisot, Payen de Montdidier and Archambaud de St Aman.[49] The cathedral was full of members of church hierarchy in their ornate clerical garb, and richly clad nobles. The Templars wore closely cropped hair, bushy beards and old, tattered clothes.

Hughes de Payens was the primary speaker at the council. His speech described the Templars' life, hardship, and purpose in Outremer. It ended with a plea for formal support from the Church, rules to live by, funds and recruits. The requests were approved by the Abbot Bernard de Clairvaux, and were accepted by all those who were present. Church acceptance was gained by the approval of Pope Honorius II. The rules to live by were detailed and harsh. They were achieved by the adoption of the original seventy-two articles of the 'Rule' of the Temple, which is also known as the 'Latin Rule' or the 'Primitive Rule'.[50] Funds and recruits came in as Hughes de Payens toured Europe and the British Isles.

The Council of Troyes also laid the foundation for the elements that were to become the cause of the Templars' downfall. It was at the council that the Templars initially received the blessing of the Pope. This ultimately led to the Templars becoming responsible only to the Pope, and free and autonomous from secular authority. The evolution of the Templars somewhat follows the saying that originated with Lord Acton: 'Power tends to corrupt, and absolute power corrupts absolutely.'[51] As the Templars gained autonomy and wealth, they became ever more powerful, and more arrogant. This arrogance was as evident in Scotland as it was in mainland Europe.

At the conclusion of the Council of Troyes the Templars possessed an immense amount of stature, and access to what was to become their overwhelming wealth. But even with the land and money provided by the kings and nobles, there are still those who question how the Templars acquired their wealth. And this question goes back to the Templars' excavations beneath what had been the Temple of Solomon. Some speculate that what they found in the catacombs of the temple was what motivated the Pope to grant the Order its unique and extensive rights. Along with the speculation of riches, there is also a theory that the Templars discovered a credible set of documents, including gospels, which refuted the canonical gospels of Matthew, Mark, Luke and John. But this overlooks a number of salient facts. The Templars had the support of Bernard de Clairvaux, whose influence was significant, and of the Pope, the only earthly authority to which they answered. Also, the Templars were an independently funded permanent fighting force in Outremer. This saved the Pope and the European kings the expense of financing the permanent army. And, being monks, the Templars did not carry the stigma that had become attached to other knights. From this it appears that historians are correct when they simply describe the creation of the primitive Rule, and papal approvals beginning with the Council of Troyes, as the basis for the Templars' wealth and power.

A BRIEF DESCRIPTION OF THE ENEMY

The history of the Knights Templar is incomplete without a brief discussion and overview of the Saracens' effectiveness during the presence of the Templars in Outremer. To a great extent, the effectiveness of the Christians and the Templars was inversely proportional to Muslim unity. When the Muslim sects were splintered, the Christians prevailed in battle and controlled the population centres. But when the Muslims were united, Christian and Templar defeat would ultimately follow. The effectiveness of the Saracens can be divided into three periods of time or stages.[52]

During the first period, from 1129 to 1193, the Muslims were in abject disarray. But beginning in 1171, Salah-ad-Din Yusuf ibn Ayyub, or 'Saladin', began a campaign to unite the Muslims. Surprisingly, he was a Kurd. His first success was to unite the tribes in what is now northern Syria, and become the Sultan of Damascus. He then directed his campaign to the south and ultimately united Egypt, becoming its sultan. His campaign reached its zenith on 4 July 1187 at the Battle of Hattin, which saw the total defeat of the Christians.

During the second stage, from 1193 to 1260, Saladin's empire was divided between his brother and sons. There were a series of five- to ten-year truces between Muslims and Christians. Each of these was followed by a crusading campaign, or series of battles, and then another truce. During the truces there was no raiding and no sieges.

During the third stage, 1260–1300, the Muslims became unified under the Mamluk Egyptians. Their rise to power began after their victory over the Mongols who were invading Palestine in the 1250s and '60s. The Christian presence effectively ended with the fall of the port of Acre to the Mamluks in 1291.

THE GROWTH OF THE TEMPLARS

Even though the Knights Templar existed under papal authority, they received even greater recognition and authority from the Pope in 1135 at the Council of Pisa. Pope Innocent II repaid the Templars and Bernard de Clairvaux for their support of his papacy when he was challenged by Anacletus II of Rome. As a reward for his victory, Innocent II granted the Templars a mark of gold each year. Each of the other 113 clergy at the Council of Pisa contributed a mark of silver. This further enriched the Templar coffers and their stature. The efforts of Hughes de Payens had come to fruition, and he was able to see the result before he died on 24 May 1136.

The next significant event occurred on 29 March 1139 when Innocent II issued a papal bull titled *Omne Datum Optimum*, which was the final step in the Templars attaining absolute autonomy. The rights it granted were extensive. It granted the Knights Templar the right to appoint their own chaplains who would be responsible to the Master and not to any local bishop, the right to build their own churches[53] and the right to receive tithes.[54] Pope Innocent II, in essence, declared that the Templars were not only an autonomous military order, but gave them the power to become an international conglomerate not subject to borders or taxation.

The year of 1139 was also significant because by then the Templars had solidified their presence in Outremer by building a number of fortifications. The type of construction of the early fortifications is unknown because at that time the Templars did not have the funds necessary to build stone castles, but rather built their defenses behind such things as earthen berms. They began in the north at La Roche de Roussel, north of Antioch in what is now the southernmost part of Turkey near the Syrian border. Just south of that was the castle of Darbsak. A little further south was the fort at Baghras which guarded the Belen Pass into Syria. Further south, on the Mediterranean coast, was the fort of Port Bonnet. Near 'Atlit, the Templars took over the castle at Destroit – which was near the road to Mount Carmel – to assist in the protection of pilgrims. Also, in 1139 Eleanor of Aquitaine (then the wife of Louis VII of France) gave the Templars certain mills, buildings and enclosures in the port of La Rochelle, free of customs, infractions and levies.[55] La Rochelle became the Templars' most important port on the Atlantic coast, and it is believed that La Rochelle was the destination and the shipping point for the Templar treasure that was transported out of Paris prior to the Templars' arrest on 13 October 1307.

Milites Templi was a subsequent papal bull issued in 1144 by Pope Celestine II which was almost an exact repeat of *Omne Datum Optimum*.[56] *Militia Templi* added military authority for the Templar clergy to protect their persons and goods. *Militia Dei*, issued in 1145, re-enforced the Templars' right to collect tithes, obligations and burial fees.[57]

The Second Crusade, which took place between 1147 and 1149, was significant because at the Temple in Paris, prior to the Templars' departure, Pope Eugenius III gave the Templars the right to wear the red cross on their white tunics, signifying their willingness to suffer martyrdom in defense of the Holy Land. This crusade ended when the Franks failed to capture Damascus in 1148.[58] This failure is attributed by some historians to the deceit of the Templars.[59] Specifically, many historians write that the Templars had accepted a bribe from the Muslims to end the siege. But the historian William of Tyre, in the mid-1150s, would not assign blame to the Templars when the Templars were at the height of their effectiveness.[60] They were devout, they were Palestine's best warriors, and they visibly escorted thousands of pilgrims to Jerusalem and the holy sites. They were respected bankers, merchants and seamen. Because of the continuing crusades and constant flow of pilgrims, the Templars had a clear purpose. The Christians were in control of the Holy Land, and the Templars had not yet gained a reputation for secrecy and avarice. This would develop over the next several decades, and be the primary reason for their downfall over 150 years later.

The Rule was again amended in the mid-1160s to add Hierarchical Articles or *retrais*. Then in the late 1160s, the Articles on conventional life, the holding of chapters, and penance were added.

THE TEMPLARS' DECLINE AND FALL

As early as 1173 the attitude of the Templars, and the Order's values, if not their dedication and fighting abilities, had begun to change. In the beginning, the goals of the Templars were focused on saving the Holy Land. But by the 1170s the Templars had begun to look towards expanding their power, their influence and their wealth. This is demonstrated by the often told story of the murder of the Assassin envoy by the Templars. It is a story that highlights the loyalty of the Grand Master to the Knights, the Knights' focus on money, and their mistrust of others.

The Assassins were a group of twelfth- and thirteenth-century Shiite Muslims whose activities were primarily directed towards the Sunnis. They were very puritanical and believed that death was the appropriate punishment for most, if not all acts of misfeasance. Their name in Arabic is *Hashishiyun*. The name Assassins is a western term. There is a dispute as to whether before an assassination they would inhale hashish, but nevertheless they became very efficient at their craft of murder. The Assassins did, on occasion, put their services out for hire.

The event involves Amalric, the King of Jerusalem, the Assassins and the Templars. Amalric was alarmed at the rising power of Saladin, a Sunnite, and sought an alliance between the Assassins and the Templars. He and the Assassins made a number of promises. Strangely enough, the Assassins agreed to adopt the Christian faith if the Templars agreed to give up the annual tribute the Assassins paid the Templars.

The Templars did not trust King Amalric, and did not believe he would keep his word. So, rather than worry about future negotiations and the loss of income, a one-eyed Templar named Walter de Mesnil killed the Assassin envoy on their return to their mountain castle in Persia known as Alamut – the Eagle's Nest.[61] The Assassins were furious. Both King Amalric and the Assassins demanded that Walter de Mesnil be arrested and put on trial. But Odo de St Amand, the Templar Grand Master, would have none of it. He backed, and was loyal to, Walter de Mesnil, and would only allow him to be tried by the Pope in Rome. But Amalric and the Assassins were not to be denied justice. Amalric personally led the raid on Sidon where Odo de St Amand had placed Walter de Mesnil. The Templars' defenses were insufficient, and Amalric's troops gained entry, arrested Walter de Mesnil and carried him off. Apparently this appeased the Assassin Chief. Nothing more is known of Walter de Mesnil.

At the same time that Saladin gained strength, the Templar leadership became over-confident. The forces came together at the Battle of Hattin in the hills behind Tiberias near the Sea of Galilee in 1187. The Christians were soundly defeated. The loss of Jerusalem soon followed and there was a substantial diminution of the Franks' influence in Outremer.[62]

The location of the Battle of Hattin demonstrates that while the Templars were formidable warriors and businessmen, their judgement was not without fault. Hattin was a very poor, if not the worst possible site for the battle from the point of view of the Franks and Templars. Saladin's army had rested in the lush pastures of Hattin for over a day. The Franks and Templars were coming from Sephoria, a place about twelve miles away. To get to Hattin, the Christian troops had to cross arid plain under a blazing midsummer sun. At the time the first battle began, the troops were dehydrated and exhausted. The initial battle during the first day was lost. When they camped for the night, Saladin's troops were able to cut off the Templars and Franks from water. Saladin then had his troops burn what little dry grass there was around the campsite so that smoke would drift among the Franks and Templars. The situation was exacerbated by the fact that the Sea of Galilee and the surrounding green pastures could be seen from the Templar camp. Many of the troops bolted for the water. The remaining Templars fought valiantly, but without success. The rest is history.

It is agreed that the battle was the result of poor decisions by the Templar Master Garard de Rideforte. Specifically, it was his decisions that caused the Franks and the Templars to be where they were at Hattin at the time of the battle. And Garard de Rideforte is said to have given the order to begin the attack.

The defeat essentially marks the end of European rule of the Middle East. The Europeans continued to maintain a significant presence in Outremer, but they recovered only a small portion of their original conquest. They never again conquered Jerusalem. The Saracens feared and dreaded the Templars; after the Battle of Hattin, the Templars who survived were captured and taken to Saladin's palace where they were individually beheaded in front of him.

The Third Crusade, during the years 1189 and 1192, was led by Richard the Lionheart. It recovered much of Outremer along the coast, but did not reclaim Jerusalem. One of the reasons given is that the Templars argued to abandon further progress towards Jerusalem, fortify the nearby city of Ascolon and wait for a better opportunity. Another reason, and one that seems more logical, is that while the Franks were within about twelve miles of Jerusalem, they elected to stop because of the difficulty in providing long-term logistical support to a city as complex and difficult to maintain as Jerusalem. Also, by agreement, Jerusalem was opened to Christian pilgrims.

In 1191, the Templars established a new headquarters at Acre, a city north of Jerusalem on the Mediterranean Sea. It remained their headquarters or a major house for another 100 years.

During the next year the Templars occupied Cyprus, and they continued to have some form of presence there until 1571.

The Fourth Crusade, between 1202 and 1204, started with Egypt as its objective. But the Crusaders were unable to pay the Venetians for their sea transport, and they ended up sacking Constantinople which had dire historical consequences for the Byzantine Empire.[63]

Next was the 'Children's Crusade' which occurred in 1212. It was a travesty. The Templars were not involved, but it is included to demonstrate the deceit and corruption of the times. The Children's Crusade was organized by Stephen of Cloyes, a teenager. He recruited an army of teenagers to fight the Saracens with the idea that the energy of youth fighting under the Christian banner would be invincible. But the young people never arrived in Outremer because they were kidnapped and sold into slavery in Africa by the unscrupulous fleet owner.[64]

The Fifth Crusade took place in 1217 and 1218. Templar banking and letters of credit were a substantial factor in the logistical success of the Fifth Crusade, if not its military success. To finance the crusade and avoid payment problems, large sums were deposited with Haimard, the Templar treasurer, at the Temple in Paris.[65] Comparable sums were then drawn in Outremer or anywhere else where the Templars had a significant presence. Again, the Templars did not charge interest. Instead they charged 'rent' and collected fees.

These letters of credit, as they are now known, avoided the problems that occurred by physically transporting exceptionally large amounts necessary to finance a crusade to the eastern Mediterranean area. Unfortunately, the crusade lacked strong leadership, and the forces were flooded out when they were trapped in the Nile delta and forced to ignominiously retreat back to Acre.[66]

The construction of a new castle at Atlit, about twenty-five miles south of Acre, took place between 1217 and 1221 as the replacement for the castle at Destroit. Atlit is also known as Castle Pilgrim because a vast amount of pilgrim and crusader labor was used in conjunction with the Templars' masons to build it.[67] The area was very productive in terms of fisheries and agriculture. The castle and the Templar presence protected both the economic endeavors, and the pilgrims on the road to Mount Carmel. It was also built as a temporary headquarters for the Templars until they could move to a fortified Jerusalem.[68] It was one of the strongest castles in Outremer and was never captured. It and the town around it were evacuated after the fall of Acre in 1291.

The Sixth Crusade was, on the one hand, one of the most successful crusades, and on the other a pathetic comedy of errors. It occurred between 1228 and 1229. It had its origins in 1212 when Frederick II was crowned King of Germany and vowed to go on a crusade. But when he was made emperor of the Holy Roman Empire in 1220 he still had not organized it. He had not organized a crusade fifteen years later, in 1227, when his mentor, Pope Honorius, died and Gregory III succeeded him. One of the first things Gregory III did was to excommunicate Frederick II for not having carried out a crusade. In response, Frederick immediately began one. But crusades were to be carried out under the Pope's command and authority. Frederick had not obtained papal authority, nor had he made supplication to the Pope to have his excommunication removed. Because of this, the Pope again excommunicated him. As a result, Frederick arrived in Acre in September 1228 with two excommunications, and he was not at all welcome. The Christians in Outremer took their religion very seriously. The Templars owed their allegiance to the Pope.

But Frederick II was the Holy Roman Emperor, and he had brought a small, but adequate army with him. He also brought with him a level of education that was so significant that it was unknown in Europe. Frederick II had not been raised in Europe, but in Sicily, which was then, as now, half-Greek and half-Arab. He not only spoke German, but Greek, Arabic, and three other languages. He was also trained in all the then known sciences, and carried the title *stupor mundi et immutator mirabilis*, or 'marvel of the world'.

When Frederick began his march south towards Egypt, he placed both the Templars and the Sultan al-Kamil in a quandary, although each for a different reason. Because the Templars owed their allegiance to the Pope, they could not take command from an excommunicated emperor in an unauthorized crusade. But their duty was to protect travelers and Christians in Outremer. As a result, when the march began, the Templars separated themselves from Frederick's forces. This was fine until the Muslims began to successfully attack the main force. The Templars, being pragmatic, agreed to join if the orders were given in the name of God and by someone other than Frederick.

Al-Kamil's quandary was whether or not to begin another battle that would detract from his siege of Damascus. This opened the door to negotiations. In the end, Frederick obtained Christian rule for Jerusalem and other parts of the Holy Land including Nazareth and Bethlehem with safe corridors to all the sites. But even though Frederick had obtained the most significant victory after Richard the Lionheart, and one that was never again equaled, no one was happy. The Church was unhappy because Jerusalem had been won by an excommunicate. In addition, the Templars were unhappy because the treaty provided that the Muslims remain in control of the Dome on the Rock which stood over their original quarters in the catacombs under the Temple of Solomon. The result was a dispute and open hostilities between the Templars and Frederick II. The animosity finally came to an end when the Pope declared war on Frederick's holdings in Italy. Frederick had to return to Europe immediately. For all his success, Frederick did not leave Outremer with cheers and fanfare. He left amid jeering citizens that pelted him with dung and offal.

Frederick II's treaty only lasted ten years. When it expired in 1244, Jerusalem was returned to the Muslims.

The absolute trust of the Templars by the kings and nobles is demonstrated by the Seventh Crusade in 1250. The Seventh Crusade was undertaken by Louis IX to capture Cairo and southern Egypt. It began well with the capture of Damietta at the eastern Nile delta, but it soon bogged down. The city of Mansurah is about fifty miles up the Nile from Damietta and about a quarter of the way to Cairo. The Templars' Master, Guillaume de Sonne, argued to consolidate their position on the coast and take Alexandria. But Louis IX's brother, Count Robert of Artois, argued vociferously for an assault on Mansurah and then Cairo. King Louis was swayed by his brother's argument. The going was slow at first because Muslim raiders continually harassed the crusaders, and Louis would not allow retaliation. But this came to an end when a Templar was attacked. The Templar Master ordered a counter-attack which resulted in the death of hundreds of Muslims. Louis IX and his forces proceeded rapidly to Mansurah. When they arrived they found that the gates had been left open. With no resistance, the Templars and crusaders went directly to the citadel, but they soon found themselves trapped in narrow streets with the Muslim troops behind them and filling all the side streets. All of the attacking troops were killed, including over 200 Templars. The Templar Master, Guillaume de Sonne, was killed after losing an eye to an arrow. King Louis IX was captured. The enormity of the defeat was described in a report that was carried to France:

> According to the statement of the master of the Templars in Scotland, the ransom of the king of France, captured by Saracens in Egypt, amounted to 40,000 pounds. The number of those killed was 60,000, and 20,000 from the Frankish army, this was in the year 1250. This was for a long time kept secret from Lady Blanche, the King's mother and the whole baronage of France, lest in desperation they should refuse to consent to the Ransom.[69]

The name of Scotland's Master is unknown. But the story exemplifies the trust that had been earned by the Templars. The Master from

Scotland was entrusted with not only taking the message to France, and ultimately to the king's mother, but returning to Egypt with the King's ransom. The ransom was so enormous that after the Franks had gathered all available funds, they still needed substantially more. The only source available was the Templars, who had more than enough on their flagship. But when the commander was asked to release this money, he responded that it consisted of deposits, could be dispensed only to the depositors, and could only be loaned to someone other than another Templar with the consent of the Grand Master. But he had been killed, and choosing a new Master took a substantial amount of time. Marshal Renaud de Vichiers had a solution. The Franks could 'take' the money and then it would not be a loan. So another one of King Louis' brothers, Count John de Joinville, boarded the Templar flagship, and with an axe threatened to break into one of the chests. With that, the Marshal handed de Joinville the key, and he took the money necessary to complete the ransom.

Interesting conclusions can be drawn from this episode. The Templars would not deviate from the strict observance of the Rule. But, at the same time, they were not above bending the Rule to fit the circumstances. For example, the king had more than enough money on deposit with the Templars in Acre to cover the alleged theft. The Templars held immense wealth; when he threatened to steal the money, de Joinville apparently threatened to break open only one of many chests.

In the years prior to 1291, European interest in Outremer had waned. Except for another unsuccessful attempt by Philip IX, there were no more crusades. The Europeans were trading with the Arabs. The secular nobility turned many of its castles over to the Templars because it did not have the funds to support them. And even the Templar holdings diminished because of the lack of European support. But the Templars were still a significant military and economic force. Prior to 1291 there were more than 970 Templar houses, including commanderies and castles, in both east and west. These were serviced by an estimated membership (including knights, sergeants, associates and chaplains) of over 7,000. In addition to this were an estimated 50,000 dependents and employees.[70] This was an immense support system for the Templars' efforts in the Holy Land. But unfortunately this empire, so to speak, was declining, or was being retained in what would today be called a maintenance mode.

After the Battle of Hattin, the Templars' primary house and headquarters were at the town and fort at Acre, which is about fifteen miles north of the modern Israeli port of Haifa. Acre was built on a promontory in the Mediterranean Sea and had been impregnable. But by 1291 all the land around Acre was in the hands of the Mamluks, and the city fell to them in three days, from 16 to 18 May 1291. The fall of Acre ended the European presence in Outremer and was followed by the evacuation of the cities of Tortosa and Atlit. All that remained was the isle of Ruad just two miles off the coast of what is today northern Syria.

The Templars at Ruad held out until 1302, hoping to use the island as a staging area for another crusade. Stephen Howarth states that they left because their Order was coming under attack from fellow Christians in the west.[71] Malcolm Barber claims the island and the Templars were starved into submission when they were attacked by a fleet of sixteen ships sent by the Mamluks.[72] Regardless of why the Templars departed, this was the very last European outpost in Outremer. With the loss of the Holy Land came the loss of the Templars' purpose. In modern parlance, the Templars were ripe for a 'hostile takeover'. And that is exactly what happened five years later.

ARRESTS AND TRIAL

On 14 September 1307 Philip IV of France (Philip le Bel [the Fair]) made a number of charges against the Templars. Specifically, the charges were made by Esquiu de Florian and were basically that:

a. the Templars put their Order and its welfare before every moral and religious principle, and took oath to defend and enrich it, whether right or wrong;
b. they kept up a secret correspondence with the Moslems;
c. novices on admission were required to spit on the cross, to renounce Christ, and to take part in a mock ceremonial;
d. any who attempted to expose the Order were secretly murdered;
e. the Templars despised the sacraments of the Church, omitted the words of consecration in the canon of the Mass, and practiced lay absolution and idolatry;
f. they were addicted to immorality and sodomy;

g. they had betrayed the Holy Land;

h. they worshipped the devil, usually in the form of a cat.

Philip IV then ordered that the Templars' land and wealth be seized and the Templars themselves arrested and imprisoned. Historians are unanimous in the view that most of the charges were trumped up. As is discussed in a later chapter, Philip the Fair had a number of ulterior motives. For example, he had sought to become a Knight Templar and had been turned down. He was deeply in debt to the Templars, and was displeased with the fact that he could not tax their land.

The Templars were arrested by King Philip on Friday 13 October 1307.[73] Because much has been written about the trials and the torture of the Templars, a lengthy discussion will not be entered into here.[74] It is agreed that most of the charges were false. Many of those who were arrested did confess, but the torture of those times was excruciatingly brutal. The following is a short, contemporary description of what happened:

> They were arrested without warning, suddenly, without right, and without any judgment being made against them. They were shamefully and dishonorably incarcerated with destructive rage, afflicted with taunts, the gravest threats, and various sorts of torture, compelled to die or produce absurd lies which they knew nothing about, wrongly given into the hands of their enemies, who force them through those torments to read out a foul, filthy and lying list which cannot be conceived by human ears and should not enter the human heart. But when the brothers refuse to produce these lies, although they know absolutely nothing about them, the torments of the attendants who press them daily force them to speak the lies, saying that they must recite them before the Jacobins [the Dominican friars who interrogated them] and assert that they are true if they wish to preserve their lives and obtain the King's plentiful grace.[75]

According to this anonymous friend of the Order, writing in Paris in early 1308, thirty-six brothers in Paris died under torture rather than confess, while many others elsewhere in France had also died. He declared that these brothers were martyrs and now had their reward in Heaven. But the Dominican friars and others involved in the interrogation refused to listen to the brothers' insistence that all these charges were false, and continued to torture them until either they confessed or died.[76]

Regarding those who did confess, there is little dispute that the vast majority of the French Templars were middle-aged members of the European support network, with little or no combat experience, who quickly confessed under torture, or the threat of it, by the Dominican friars who were put in charge of the interrogations. The cruelty they faced from Philip IV, the Pope and the inquisition is demonstrated by the burning of fifty-four Templars as relapsed heretics near Paris in 1310. Facing this threat, the result is consistent with what happened to the astronomer Galileo Galilei who, in 1633, under threat of torture by Dominican friars, recanted all of his scientific discoveries and submitted himself to a lifetime of house arrest. In fact, many Templars who did not confess were burned at the stake, as depicted in a fourteenth-century painting in Figure 2.

During 1311 and 1312 Pope Clement V held the Council of Vienna. On 22 March 1312 he issued the papal bull *Vox in excelso* which abolished the Knights Templar.[77] On 2 May 1312 he issued an additional papal bull *Ad providam* which transferred all Templar property to the Hospitallers.[78]

Jacques de Molay, the Templars' last Grand Master before their dissolution, is depicted in Figure 3. He and his Seneschal, Geoffroi of Charney, were executed on 18 March 1314. They were burned to death on an island in the Seine close to Notre-Dame while King Philip IV looked on. Prior to his death, Jacques de Molay called for the judgement of God on both Philip and Pope Clement V. Legend has it that king and Pope were cursed by Jacques de Molay, who vowed that neither would live out the year. Neither did.

The charges of heresy are easily countered by an examination of the Templars' practices and by their adherence to the Rule. During August 1308 three cardinals were sent by Pope Clement V to hold hearings at Chinon Castle to learn the guilt or innocence of the Templars. The cardinals found the Templars innocent. The Templars were absolved by the cardinals in a document found in the archives of the Vatican known as the Chinon Parchment.[79]

Individually the Knights Templar lived in poverty. They 'owned' no personal possessions, and lived what we would call a spartan existence. Yet as an organization, they possessed wealth that was the envy of

Europe. They were the finest warriors in the world, yet it appears that their numbers and wealth created an inevitable bureaucracy that was part of their undoing. They were willing to die for their beliefs. But with this ultimate sacrifice there was an arrogance that also contributed to the end of the Order as it existed throughout Europe and the British Isles.

Legend has it that prior to 13 October 1307 Jacques de Molay ordered that the treasure held in the Paris Temple be shipped out of France; much of it was shipped to Portugal, but most, it seems, was shipped to Scotland.

There is little dispute that many of the Templars and much of their treasure escaped to Portugal. In Portugal, the Knights Templar became the 'Knights of Christ'.[80] But there is still some disagreement about how it happened. Laurence Gardner states that in Portugal in 1307, the Knights Templar became reincorporated as the 'Knights of Christ'.[81] But Malcolm Barber says that 'after the Temple was suppressed in 1312 the new order of Christ [Knights of Christ] created by King Diniz of Portugal in 1319 was largely based upon Templar property and personnel'.[82]

There is also dispute as to whether the Templars and their treasure were transported out of France to Scotland. The evidence that is discussed in later chapters indicates that they were. But Stephen Howarth has an insightful evaluation of the status of the Templars in Scotland after 1307:

> Scotland is intriguing, however, for although in the last, terrible days only two Templars were arrested there, the country contained a substantial quantity of Templar property. Around Aberdeen alone, their cross stood on houses and churches in Turriff, Tullich, Maryculter, Aboyne and Kingcausie. In Aberdeen itself they had a chapel, recorded in 1907 as 'lying between Dancing Master Peacock's close and Gardener's Lane'; and south of the town, at Culter, they had an estate of no less than eight thousand acres. Clearly there must have been more than two men to run all these; but what became of these men – no one knows. There are traditions of escaped Templars and secret preceptories in the outer isles; but these are fantasies born centuries after the Order's suppression; there are no facts on which to base them.[83]

If the legend/theory is correct, and Mr Howarth is not, there is still a substantial divergence as to where in Scotland the Templars' treasures were initially shipped. One view favors the Inner Hebrides and Argyll.

Another favors the Orkney Islands which were held by the Sinclairs. There are also those who posit that such treasure as did exist was ultimately hidden in the vaults under the Rosslyn Chapel.

Support for a Templar presence in Scotland after 1307 is found in the books by Michael Baigent and Richard Leigh, and by Tim Wallace-Murphy and Marilyn Hopkins.[84] But the arguments by these authors have been the subject of various levels of criticism. But even if the arguments have fault, the premises of the authors may not. After 1312 the Templars continued to keep an archive in Cyprus. Unfortunately it was destroyed by the Ottomans in 1571.

NOTES

1　There are myths that state the Templars were formed in France prior to the First Crusade, and that their true purpose was not to protect pilgrims, but to explore the catacombs under the remnants of the Temple of Solomon in Jerusalem. There are no known facts to support these myths. They arise, in part, from the questions that are raised later in this chapter.

2　Burnes, James, *Sketch of the History of the Knights Templars*, Wm. Blackwood & Sons (Edinburgh, 1840), p. 10. Burnes devotes an entire chapter to the continuation of the Knights Templar after it was allegedly abolished in 1307–12.

3　The Temple of Solomon was first built by King Solomon in 950 BCE on what is known as the Temple Mount in Jerusalem. It was destroyed by the Chaldeans in 586, but rebuilt in 515 BCE Beginning around 30 BCE Herod rebuilt the Temple and expanded it to a scale that was exceptional for the time. In 70 CE the Romans put down a rebellion in Palestine that included the Jews. In their recapture of Jerusalem, the Romans totally destroyed this Second Temple. Only portions of the catacombs remained.

4　For examples, see: Wallace-Murphy, Tim & Hopkins, Marilyn, *Rosslyn, Guardian of the Secrets of the Holy Grail*, Element Books Limited (Shaftesbury, 1999), p. 114; Gardner, Laurence, *Bloodline of the Holy Grail*, Barnes & Noble (New York, 1997), p. 258; Sanello, Frank, *The Knights Templar, God's Warriors, the Devil's Bankers*, Taylor Trade Publishing (Lanham, 2003), p. 4; Sora, Steven, *The Lost Treasure of the Knights Templar*, Destiny Books (Rochester, 1999), pp. 37–38, 124–126.

5　Nicholson, Helen, *The Knights Templar: A New History*, Sutton Publishing Ltd (Gloucestershire, 2001), p. 42.

6 Barber, Malcolm, *The Trial of the Templars*, Canto edition, Cambridge University Press (Cambridge, 1993).

7 Partner, Peter, *The Knights Templar and their Myth*, Destiny Books (Rochester, Vermont, 1990), p. 6.

8 'In Praise of the New Knighthood, *Liber as milites Templi: De laude novae militae*', translated by Lisa Coffin, in Wasserman, James, *The Templars and the Assassins, The Militia of Heaven*, Inner Traditions (Rochester, Vermont, 2001), pp. 278, 284.

9 Barber, Malcolm, *The New Knighthood, A History of the Order of the Temple*, Canto ed., Cambridge University Press (Cambridge, 1994), p. 15.

10 Picket, Lynn & Prince, Clive, *The Templar Revelation*, Touchstone, Simon & Schuster (New York, 1998), pp. 97–98.

11 Upton-Ward, J.M., *The Rule of the Templars*, The Boydell Press (Suffolk, 1992). All references to the Rule are from this book. Rule, Art. 21.

12 Rule, Art. 26.

13 Rule, Art. 23, 31–32.

14 Rule, Art. 48.

15 Rule, Art. 43.

16 Rule, Art. 304. It is interesting to note that while the prayer schedule was started by the Cistercian and Benedictine monks, it is currently followed at certain times by not only the clergy of the Catholic Church, but by that of the Lutherans, Anglicans/Episcopalians and other early Protestant religions.

17 Rule, Art. 11.

18 Robinson, John J., *Born in Blood, the Lost Secrets of Freemasonry*, M. Evens & Co. (New York, 1989), pp. 71–72.

19 Barber, *The New Knighthood*, pp. 6–7.

20 Howarth, Stephen, *The Knights Templar*, Barns & Noble (New York, 1992), p. 245.

21 Rule, Art. 77 *et seq.*

22 Rule, Art. 99 *et seq.*

23 Rule, Art. 101 *et seq.*

24 Rule, Art. 110 *et seq.*

25 Rule, Art. 120 *et seq.*

26 Rule, Art. 130 *et seq.*

27 See the Rule at Articles 51 and 57.

28 Rule, Art. 65–66.

29 Rule, Art. 68.

30 Rule, Art. 268–271. Papal bull of Alexander III *Omne Datum Optimum*.

31 Rule, Art. 175, 319, 321 *et seq.*

32 Barber, *The New Knighthood,* p. 14. Howarth, *The Knights Templar,* p. 64. Frale, Barbara, *The Knights Templar, The Secret History Revealed,* Arcade Publishing (New York, 2009), p. 30.

33 Howarth, *The Knights Templar,* p. 65.

34 Ibid., p. 234.

35 Butler, Alan & Dafoe, Stephan, *The Warriors and the Bankers,* Templar Books (Canada, 1998), p. 27, refers to the Knights Templar as 'Templar Inc.'

36 Rule, Art. 325.

37 Rule, Art. 61, 190–197.

38 Rule, Art. 61.

39 The preceptory of Denney in Cambridgeshire was a hospital for sick and elderly brothers, as was the preceptory at Eagle in Lincolnshire. Burman, Edward, *The Templars, Knights of God,* Destiny Books (Rochester, Vermont, 1986), p. 95. Parker, Thomas W., *The Knights Templars in England,* University of Arizona Press (Tucson, 1963), p. 41.

40 Baigent, Leigh and Lincoln, *The Holy Blood and the Holy Grail,* Jonathan Cape (1982), pp. 67–68.

41 Rule, Art. 443; Barber, *The New Knighthood,* pp. 217–218.

42 Rule, Art. 34.

43 Rule, Art. 29.

44 Rule, Art. 24, 29.

45 Rule, Art. 74.

46 Rule, Art. 15–16.

47 Rule, Art. 28.

48 Rule, Art. 30.

49 Upton-Ward, *The Rule of the Templars,* p. 3.

50 The Rule was expanded several times to a total of 685 articles.

51 Letter to Bishop Creighton, 1887.

52 Nicholson, *The Knights Templar: A New History,* pp. 48–50.

53 Howarth, *The Knights Templar,* p. 80.

54 Partner, *The Knights Templar and their Myth,* p. 3. Rule, Art. 58.

55 Barber, *The New Knighthood,* pp. 25–26.

56 Howarth, *The Knights Templar,* p. 83.

57 Barber, *The New Knighthood,* p. 58.

58 Hallam, *Chronicles of the Crusades,* CLB International (1989), pp. 143–146. The term 'Franks' originally referred to a Rhineland Germanic tribe, but during the Crusades, in Outremer, it generally referred to western

Europeans. Ralls, Karen, *Knights Templar Encyclopedia*, New Age Books (Franklin Lakes, 2007), p. 69.

59 Ibid., p. 148.

60 Nicholson, *The Knights Templar: A New History*, p. 74. Barbara Frale, *The Knights Templar*, p. 95 goes so far as to laud the Templars' performance.

61 Howarth, *The Knights Templar*, pp. 127–128. He opines that the Templars preferred hard cash to a dubious alliance; Barber, op. cit., p. 101; Simon, Edith, *The Piebald Standard, A Biography of the Knights Templar*, Little, Brown & Co. (Boston, 1959), pp. 101–102.

62 See Howarth, *The Knights Templar*, pp. 145–156. A full description of the slaughter of the Christians at Hattin is beyond the scope of this chapter. According to Stephen Howarth, tradition holds that the Twin Peaks of Hattin above the battlefield was the site of the Sermon on the Mount. Howarth, *The Knights Templar*, p. 153.

63 Barber, *The New Knighthood*, p. 126.

64 Sora, *The Lost Treasure of the Knights Templar*, Destiny Books (1999), p. 99.

65 Barber, *The New Knighthood*, p. 127.

66 Read, Piers Paul, *The Templars*, St Martins Press (New York, 1999), p. 199.

67 Simon, *The Piebald Standard*, p. 117.

68 Howarth, *The Knights Templar*, p. 195. The east wall of Atlit is a significant example of Templar masonry. One of the obvious arguments supporting the belief that the Knights Templar were the precursors to the Masons is the fact that masons were heavily involved with building the Templars' numerous churches and forts.

69 MacQuarrie, Alan, *Scotland and the Crusades, 1095–1560*, John Donald Publishers, Ltd (Edinburgh, 1985), p. 49; quoting from Matthew Paris, *Chronica Maiora*, vi, 521.

70 Barber, M., 'Supplying the Crusader States', in *The Horns of Hattin*, edited by B.Z. Kedar (Jerusalem: Yad Izhak Ben-Zvi; Aldershot: Ashgate Variorum, 1992), p. 186.

71 Howarth, *The Knights Templar*, p. 229.

72 Barber, *The New Knighthood*, p. 294.

73 This is believed to be *the* Friday the 13th that we all think about twice a year.

74 See: Barber, Malcolm, *The Trial of the Templars*.

75 Nicholson, *The Knights Templar: A New History*, p. 217, quoting from C.R. Cheney, 'The Downfall of the Templars and a Letter in their Defense', p. 323.

76 Ibid., p. 217.

77 Howarth, *The Knights Templar*, p. 305.

78 Barber, *The New Knighthood*, p. 304.

79 Frale, Barbara, *The Knights Templar: The Secret History Revealed*, Arcade Publishing (New York, 2009), p. 3.

80 Gardner, *Bloodline of the Holy Grail*, pp. 271, 294.

81 Ibid., pp. 271, 294.

82 Barber, *The New Knighthood*, p. 34.

83 Howarth, op. cit., p. 243.

84 Baigent & Leigh, *The Temple and the Lodge*, Arcade Publishing (1989), and Wallace-Murphy & Hopkins, *Rosslyn, Guardian of the Secrets of the Holy Grail*.

2

BALANTRODOCH: THE LIFE OF THE TEMPLARS

Scotland possesses no tangible memorial of its Templars. All of its temples and preceptories have vanished. Only the name remains. Templar life in Scotland between 1129 and 1309 must be constructed from articles and documents that relate to locations or events such as the Templars' headquarters in Scotland, or their real estate transactions. Surprisingly, these two subjects provide a wealth of information. Balantrodoch is important because it was the focal point of Templar activity in Scotland. It was the administrative and economic center. It was the location of the Templars' primary chapel. It remained the center for Templar activity even after the formal dissolution of the Templars in 1312; it remained a community's kirk until 1849, long after the Templars and Hospitallers were divested of their properties during the Reformation.

BALANTRODOCH

What is now the small village of Temple, a few miles south of Edinburgh, was at one time the Templars' headquarters in Scotland. It was begun by the efforts of Hughes de Payens when he undertook the expansion of The Poor Fellows–Soldiers of Jesus Christ and the Temple of Solomon from the original nine knights to an international Order. His efforts went beyond the continent of Europe to England, and all the way to Scotland and the Court of King David I.

Although the towns of Temple and Roslin are only a few miles apart, few people have heard of Temple or of Balantrodoch. This is due in large part to a small chapel just south of Edinburgh known as Rosslyn Chapel, which is highlighted in Dan Brown's very popular novel, *The Da Vinci Code*.[1] The Knights Templar gained immediate recognition because of a statement at the beginning of Chapter 104 which states that Rosslyn Chapel was built 'by the Knights Templar in 1446' and the hint that it is the repository for the Holy Grail.[2] Others have said the Rosslyn Chapel holds the Templar mysteries and is a book in stone that enshrines for posterity the Templar ideals. From this has grown a large popular interest, and tourists flock there. Whether any of this is true is the subject of Chapter 9. Suffice it to say, Rosslyn Chapel totally eclipses Balantrodoch. But in its time, Balantrodoch was not just a church. It was the focal point of Templar activity with numerous buildings and activities. It, and Scotland, were the Templar lands most distant from Jerusalem. They were cold, remote, and they provided the Templars with only minimal income.

There are various versions of the events leading up to the meeting of Hughes de Payens and King David I. Some attribute it to a relationship between de Payens and the Saint Clairs. Others base it on his very successful meeting with King Henry I of England. The connection between de Payens and the Saint Clairs begins with the premise that before the founding of the Knights Templar, Hughes de Payens was married to Catherine de Saint-Clair of the Norman line of the family.[3] From this, everything falls into place to support the idea of a Templar–Saint Clair relationship from prior to 1118 through the time they were dissolved by Pope Clement V in 1312 and after. This premise also provided a means of introduction to Scotland's king, David I. But this marriage may not have happened. The foundation for the premise is not that clear. It seems that Hughes de Payens may actually have been married to Elizabeth de Chappesm, and not to Catherine de Saint-Clair.[4] If this is true, then there is no other evidence that Hughes de Payens was introduced to David I by the Saint Clairs. In all probability, the introduction originated with Henry I, King of England.

The evidence for how and when Balantrodoch was transferred to the Templars varies. The most credible version begins with Hughes de Payens' intense campaign for recruits and money after the Council of Troyes. As part of his campaign he traveled to Normandy where he was received by Henry I who presented him with gifts of gold and silver.[5] But of greater importance is the fact that King Henry I gave Hughes de Payens his support, which included an introduction to David I of Scotland. Hughes de Payens was very well received by David I, and as part of the largesse bestowed upon the Templars were the lands that became known as Balantrodoch, or *Baile nan Trodach* – 'Stead of the Warriors'.[6] This name is believed to have followed *Baile nan Trachaid* (Traghad), 'Stead of the Seashore', from the gravel bed left by a glacier near the village of Temple. The name was changed to Stead of Warriors when it was acquired by the Templars.

At the time of the gift, David I had only been on the Scottish throne for four years. The extent of his trust and devotion to the Templars is demonstrated by the fact that he kept them around him constantly and made them judges and advisors of his conduct 'by night and day'.[7] As David's trust in the Templars grew, they became a source of candidates for the king's almoner, a person who was considered to be a man of the world and thus a judge of character, and qualified to give aid to those in real distress.[8]

Another version has it that Hughes de Payens traveled to Scotland in the summer of 1228, before the Council of Troyes and before he met with David I in Scotland.[9] In this version he was traveling throughout Europe and England to gather wealth and recruits in order to gain more influence at the Council of Troyes. This version has a basis because there is a surviving letter of thanks to David I from Bernard de Clairvaux dated June 1128. The possibility is not far-fetched because of the proximity of the nearby Cistercian Abbey of Newbattle. But, there is also the explanation that the letter does not predate the Council of Troyes, because in the Middle Ages the new year began in March.

Finally, it is often stated that David I granted the manor and chapel at Balantrodoch to the Templars when they were introduced into Scotland in 1153. But this view is primarily supported by the fact that the Templars' activity in Scotland substantially increased in the early 1150s. Also, even though Balantrodoch was the principle preceptory of Scotland, there are few records. But the name of the preceptory is well established. It is found in both the Chartulary of Aberdeen, 'a domus Templi de Balantradock', and the Chartulary of the Cistercian Abbey of Newbattle, 'Magister et Fratres Templi de Blentrodoch'.[10]

Balantrodoch is located about eleven miles south of Edinburgh on the South Esk River. It is only a few miles from the village of Roslin, and four miles from the Cistercian Abbey of Newbattle. The temple is on a ridge above the river. Foundations for pillars have been found in the garden next to the current church ruin that are believed to be from the original Templar church. It was round like the other Templar churches, and the Church of the Holy Sepulcher in Jerusalem. But Balantrodoch was not just a temple. It would have consisted of a hall with a kitchen, administration buildings, housing for the knights, sergeants/baillis and staff, a stable and a barn, outbuildings and a mill which ground all the grain from the Templar properties in the region, including wheat from Liston. By the middle of the thirteenth century, with additional grants from Alexanders II and III, its lands extended down the Esk River to Carrington and Harvieston, and up towards the Moorfoot Hills, by Halkerston, Utterston, Rosebery, and Yorkston. Because it was in the middle of lands held by the Saint Clairs, the proximity is used as support for the theory that the Saint Clairs were actively involved in the Templars' acquisition of Balantrodoch. But this goes back to the question of whether Hughes de Payens was married to Catherine de Saint-Clair. It is more probable that the Templars and the Saint Clairs were better described as neighbors and close business associates. The location of Balantrodoch is also used to support the theory that the Saint Clairs built Rosslyn Chapel, in part, to hide the Templar treasure that was transported out of Paris before the arrest of the Templars on Friday 13 October 1307. But, as with the wedding and the facts surrounding the acquisition of the property at Balantrodoch, the story has two or more versions.[11]

Regardless of how or when it was acquired, after 1229 Balantrodoch was the Templars' main preceptory in Scotland. But because Scotland never rose to a level of province, the Templars and their land in Scotland were governed by the Master of England who governed from the Temple in London.

Another bitter irony involves the work that was carried out at Balantrodoch. In the 1200s the monks at Newbattle Abbey are said to have been mining coal and producing iron. Given the relationship between the Cistercian monks, the closeness of their abbey to Balantrodoch, and the Templars' proclivity for making money to support their efforts in Outremer, one would think that these activities would also have been carried out by the Templars. But apparently they were not; instead, their primary economic activities were agriculture and the operation of the mill.

In addition to governing the Order in Scotland, Balantrodoch was the center for carrying out the Order's business. Major payments to and by the Order were made there. Charters relating to the Templars' lands were granted at Balantrodoch, and legal documents affecting Templar properties were usually signed there. The documents were drafted by clerks, who could either be brethren or employees who were not members of the Order. Major disputes were settled there, as were appointments to offices.

The Templars in Scotland were not bankers. Banking was done at the London Temple, which has been described as a thirteenth-century Bank of England. The London Temple was used by the kings of Scotland as well as the English kings and nobility.[12] For example, in 1225 Queen Ermengarde, the widow of William the Lion, bought property in order to found the monastery of Balmerinoch. The deeds for the monastery were deposited in the London Temple and held there until the money was paid. The exchange then also took place there. In another transaction, Roger le Bigod paid 2,000 pounds of silver on behalf of King Alexander II at the London Temple. Then, in 1282, Alexander III paid a debt there. Alexander III also used the London Temple to handle the payment of the dowry for his sister Isabella.

The use of the Temple in London is consistent with evidence given at the Scottish inquisition, when the knights stated that all of the Templars in Scotland were born in England. But, when one became a Templar, one lost his nationality and became a soldier of Christendom and not of any particular country or kingdom.[13] In fact, Scottish Templars served in France and Cyprus, as well as the Holy Land.[14]

The hierarchy at Balantrodoch was the same as at any other Templar preceptory. There were only two basic levels of Templars: the knights, who wore the white tunic with the red Templar cross, and the sergeants, who took the Templar vows but wore the Templar cross on a black or brown robe. They served as esquires, tending the horses and working the fields or mills at the preceptories. The other level was the chaplains, ordinary ecclesiastics who had been admitted to the Order so they could perform services and administer the sacrament to the brethren.[15] The Templars in Scotland, like all the others, were bound to the daily observance of all the canonical hours, from Matins in the early morning to Compline before they went to bed. In the refectory they ate their meal in silence while someone read from the scripture or a sacred legend. Four days a week they abstained from meat. Wine was used sparingly. On Fridays they ate nothing but Lenten food and drink. Conversation was forbidden after the brethren left the refectory. It was undoubtedly a frustratingly austere life considering that there were no battles and little, if any, need for weapons. The Templars were businessmen and absentee farmers who would be described today as upper-middle management, but without the perks that would come with such a position.

Unlike the preceptories in England, there were no inventories taken for Balantrodoch and Maryculter during the Templars' arrest and inquisition. But because the Templar Knights in Scotland were Englishmen, who were transferred from England to Scotland and back, it can be assumed that the lifestyles were comparable. And the Templars lived frugally; the hall would contain simple tables, chairs and a washbasin. The living chamber would be a dormitory with a bed and a clothes bag for each Templar. For eating, each person might have a spoon. Even this might have been generous; in Denny, eastern England, there was only one spoon for every two Templars. In terms of goods and cash, only a small amount was kept on hand.[16] The Templar Knights were not known to be terribly literate, and it appears that they kept no books other than service manuals.[17] Judging from the chapel inventory at the preceptory at Denny in eastern England, it appears that the chapel would have been well supplied with such things as vestments, cloths, chalices, cruets, and religious books.[18]

While the knights were unable to personally enjoy the fruits of their labor, the preceptory enjoyed numerous privileges. The Templars were exempt from *scot* (taxes and assessments), *gild* (membership), from attendance at the king's host and in his courts, from the casualties of ward and relief, and from all services connected with the royal castles, fleets, parks and houses.[19] In 1180, among other Templar privileges was the right to have one man, called a *hospes*, in each borough. The *hospes* would hold his Templar toft or tenement (fenced dwellings and outbuildings) in fee and heritage 'as freely and quietly, fully and honourable, as any burgess holding of us holds and possess any donation [*elemosinam*] granted to us'.[20] The extensive privileges are set forth at length in the charter of King Alexander which confirms those granted by Kings David I, Malcolm IV and William I, and includes 'buying and selling their merchandise everywhere, free of cain (livestock or produce from the land paid as rent), toll and passage-duty, and all other freights and customs'.[21]

Special privileges of this kind, while evidence of early popularity, gradually incited general antipathy. Pushed to their extreme limits, the existence of these privileges caused the emergence of powerful enemies who were banded together by envy. As the early glamor of the crusades wore off, the laity became indifferent; crusading ceased to be a source of inspiration. Even the Church began to accommodate itself to the gradually changing views. For example, it granted exemptions on somewhat easy terms to those who had taken Templar vows and afterwards changed their minds. Caesarius of Heisterback narrates the tale of a miller who, after becoming a Templar, bought himself out of the Order by paying five marks. When he learned that he might have had to pay forty marks, he had to brag about it at the local tavern:

> Ye fools will cross the seas and waste your substance and expose your lives to manifold dangers, while I shall sit at home with my wife and children, and get a like reward to yours through the five marks with which I redeemed my cross.

But the miller should have kept his mouth shut because a short time later he received his comeuppance. He was forced to ride on a coal black horse without food or water in the company of a swarthy individual mounted on an equally sable steed. He died in three days, 'and thus unrepentant, unconfessed, unanointed and unaneled', declares the chronicler, 'He found his grave in hell'. Also, the priest forbade him a Christian burial, but ultimately had his own shortcomings because he took a bribe from the miller's wife to lay him in the churchyard. The priest's bribe was discovered and he was accused in the Synod of Utrecht and received his punishment.[22]

The house at Balantrodoch, and probably the one at Maryculter were undoubtedly built in the same style as those in England which were half-baronial, half-monastic type structures.[23] They would have had strongly fortified towers, an enceinte enclosing a stately hall which served as a refectory, and a chapel which, like that of the Temple in London, appears to have been circular.

Balantrodoch is among the few Templar relics that remain on Scottish soil. While its temple was undoubtedly circular, it would have been considerably more modest than the London Temple. Unfortunately, it was substantially remodeled by the Hospitallers after 1308, and by the Protestants after the Reformation. As a result, it is now a rectangular, single-celled chapel that is eighteen feet wide by fifty-five feet long.

At no period in time were there many Templar Knights in Scotland. Generally there were from three to five knights, and about the same number of chaplains. Extrapolating from the information from England there were usually around 100 sergeants out of a total of 141 Templars in London. This means there would have been about 25 to 30 sergeants in Scotland.[24] With no known records it is impossible to be certain, but these numbers are consistent with the personnel needed to manage in excess of 600 properties in Scotland. At the time of the Templars' arrest in Scotland there were four known knights: Walter de Clifton the Preceptor, William de Middleton, and two others who fled, John de Huseflete and Thomas Totti, né Tocci (who later gave himself up).[25]

The Scottish Chief of Balantrodoch was usually a Master, but in the absence of a Master, he was the Preceptor of the House of the Temple of Scotland. His territory was bounded in the south by the River Tweed and extended to the northernmost tip of Scotland. The Masters/Preceptors were not independent, and they were not linked to France. They owed their allegiance to the Master in London. Further, the known Masters were not Scots, but Englishmen. As long as Scotland was at peace with England, everything was fine. Consider that David I made both the local monks and the Templars the 'custodians of his morals'.[26] But when disputes arose between England and Scotland, the Templars initially sided with the English.

The names of only a few Masters/Preceptors are known, and the information is not always consistent. The following are the known Preceptors at Balantrodoch.[27]

Robert	1160
Bartholomew	1165–1169[28]
Ranulph de Corbet	1174–99
Hughes de Conyers	*c.* 1233
Roger de Akiney	1278–90
Brian de Jay	1286–92
John de Sautre	1292– ?
John de Huseflete	1304–06
Walter de Clifton	1306–09

In 1240 the Templar Master was Patrick, Earl of Dunbar, who died in Marseilles on the way to the Egyptian crusade. But another Templar Master, whose name is unknown, also left Scotland to participate in the Egyptian crusade. He did take part in it, and is listed by his title as the one who facilitated the payment of the ransom for King Louis.[29]

When the Templars were dissolved, and the inquisition was announced, John de Huseflete fled. He may have been followed by William de Middleton, another Englishman, who identified himself at the inquisition as a Preceptor.

Of all Scotland's Masters, the one that is most prominent is Brian de Jay. Brian de Jay and his successor John de Sautre were both Englishmen. Both were killed at Falkirk fighting for King Edward I against William Wallace. There is an oft-repeated story involving Brian de Jay, a widow and an estate at Esperston that begins before Brian de Jay was the Master of Balantrodoch.[30] It ends in 1354 at Balantrodoch, fifty-six years after Brian de Jay's death.[31] It is often said that the events of this episode stand out as evidence of the Templars' avarice: that they were the keepers of wealth and promoters of gross injustice, instead of being the keepers of morals; that as the Templars' wealth increased, their early ideals of self-sacrifice and chivalry faded away, and were replaced by arrogance, cruelty and greed. In Scotland, as in France, it appears that it was this image that ultimately caused the Order to be brought to an end.

The story highlights the fact that the Templars were not only bankers who developed letters of credit, they also developed the concept of an annuity. The tale begins when William, the son of Geoffrey of Halkerston — who was known be fonder of ease than of labor — conveyed his wife Christiana's estate at Esperston to the Templars for the duration of his life. William was then received into the preceptory at Balantrodoch and was maintained there for the rest of his life. His wife and children then had to live in a small house at the corner of the property with a small income that barely provided them with the necessities of life. In other words, William gave the Templars a life estate. The Templars agreed to support him for life at Balantrodoch in exchange for the profits from the property.

At William's death, the small house was to be conveyed back to his wife. But it wasn't. Instead, Brian de Jay, as Master of the Temple in Scotland, took a group of his followers to the house to evict the widow and her children. She refused to leave and slammed the door in his face, claiming that her husband could not dispose of her patrimony. Not to be discouraged, Brian de Jay told his men to break in and drag her out. They did, but 'as the poor woman clung desperately with both hands to the door of her dwelling, a ruffian in the band unsheathed his dagger and cut off one of her fingers'.[32] Brian de Jay then 'took possession of the house and inheritance from which she had been iniquitously expelled'.

But the story did not end there. Later, after the widow's finger had healed, King Edward I of England was lodging nearby at Newbattle. She gained an audience and convinced the king to issue a royal writ in chancery to restore her inheritance. The widow then moved back in and lived there until the outbreak of Scotland's War of Independence. A consequence of the war was that the courts were closed. Brian de Jay took advantage of this, and the Templars again, for a second time, forcibly threw the widow out of her house.

In the summer of 1298, when Brian de Jay was in Balantrodoch with a large body of Welsh mercenaries on his way to join Edward I at Falkirk, the widow's eldest son, Richard Cook, approached Brian de Jay and pleaded his mother's cause. Brian de Jay seemed sympathetic. He promised that if Richard would lead the Welsh troops to their destination at Liston, all would be made right. Richard kept his part of the bargain, and guided the Welsh troops to their destination. But unfortunately, Brian de Jay had given a separate order to the Welsh captain to kill Richard. The following day Richard was slain. As a result the land remained in the hands of the Templars.

Brian de Jay was also killed in the Battle of Falkirk, three days after the slaying of Richard. There are several versions of how Brain de Jay met his death. One chronicler reports that he died at the start of the battle. Another states that he died charging the Scottish schiltrons. The third version has Brian de Jay chasing several Scots through a bog when his horse floundered and he was killed by the Scots he was chasing. Regardless of which version is correct, Brian de Jay met his end as a fighting knight.

The Templars retained possession of Esperston until 1312 when, during the reign of Robert the Bruce, a son of Christiana regained the property through proceedings before the Sheriff and Bailli of Edinburgh. Then, in 1354, William and Christiana's heir, Robert Semple, petitioned for restoration of his family's right to possess the estate. His petition was granted and he regained control of the family's estate. Several facts are significant. While the proceeding was civil in nature, it was not held before a civil court such as common pleas. It was conducted by the Hospitallers, but not at the preceptory of the Hospitallers which was Torphichen. Instead it took place at the Templars' preceptory at Balantrodoch by a court of thirteen men who were tenants there.[33] Also, the proceeding was conducted by Thomas de Lindesay, Master of the Knights of Saint John and the Temple.

Because there are so few records of Balantrodoch, what information there is, is anecdotal. An example is the Latin inscription that is chiseled into separate, apparently salvaged stones set into the top of the belfry or east gable of the current church, which states:

VAE SAC
IMI·HM

These letters have been the subject of much curiosity and debate after their discovery. There was no widely held understanding of it and the interpretation is still a matter of immense speculation.[34] But each of the better known interpretations is imaginative.

James Burnes in 1840 thought that the letters, when extended, might mean *Virgini Aedem Sacram Jilitia Templi Hierosolymae Magister* because the Virgin Mary was the patroness of the Order.[35]

The *Illustrated Architectural Guide to Midlothian* (1995) interprets the letters to read '*Vienne Sacrum Militibus Johannis Hierosolymitani Melitensibus*', or 'The sacred Council of Vienna to the Knights of St John of Jerusalem and Malta'.[36]

Jeff Nisbet proposed that it is a coded reference to the theory attributed to the Templars of the bloodline descending from Jesus and Mary Magdalene. He also argues that it is tied to a voyage of Henry St Clair, Earl of Orkney, to America in the late fourteenth century.[37]

THE FINAL DAYS OF THE TEMPLE

Balantrodoch appears to be one of the few Templar properties in Scotland that was actually transferred to the Hospitallers. It was after the transfer that the Temple's configuration began to change to its current rectangular shape.[38] Its name ultimately became 'Temple'. This process began before the fifteenth century when Sir William Knollis, Grand

Preceptor of the Order of St John, obtained an Act of Parliament changing the name 'Temple' to 'The Barony of St John'. But the name was not accepted by the people in the area and the name has always remained simply 'Temple'.

The Temple remained in the hands of the Knights of St John until 1535 when they lost their control because of the Protestant revolution, and specifically because of Henry VIII's Act of Reformation. After that, the chapel became the area's Protestant church. This was formalized in the next century, in 1618, when the name was changed to reflect the fact that 'Temple' applied to the area, not just the chapel. The area became known as the Parish of Temple.

The chapel was continuously used as the parish kirk until 1840. By then, because of its age and maintenance costs, it had become so dilapidated that a new church was built.

But the original chapel still stands, although, as shown in Figure 4, it is now a ruin with no roof or windows. Those who visit this peaceful and tranquil village find the remains of a stone chapel that is filled with history and memories.

NOTES

1 Doubleday (New York, 2003).

2 Brown, *The Da Vinci Code*, p. 432.

3 Sinclair, Andrew, *The Sword and the Grail*, Crown Publishers (New York, 1982). See Baigent, Michael, Leigh, Richard & Lincoln, Henry, *The Holy Blood and the Holy Grail*, Delacorte Press (New York, 1982), p. 391.

4 Coppens, Philip, *The Stone Puzzle of Rosslyn Chapel*, Frontier Publishing (Netherlands, 2004), p. 14, citing *Hugues de Payns, Chevalier Champenoise, Fondateur de l' Ordre des Templiers* (Troyes: editions de la Maison Boulanger, 1997).

5 Barber, Malcolm, *The Military Orders, Fighting for the Faith and Caring for the Sick*, Variorium, Ashgate Publishing (Hampshire, 1994), p. 143.

6 Coutts, Rev. Alfred, *The Knights Templar in Scotland* (Edinburgh, 1890), p. 7.

7 Aitken, Robert, 'The Knights Templar in Scotland', *The Scottish Review* (July 1898), p. 4.

8 Edwards, John, 'The Knights Templar in Scotland', *Transactions of the Scottish Ecclesiological Society*, Vol. IV (Aberdeen, 1912–1915), p. 41.

9 Barber, Malcolm, *The New Knighthood, A History of the Order of the Temple*, Cambridge University Press, Canto edition (New York, 1995), p. 14.

10 Burnes, James, *Sketch of the History of the Knights Templars*, 2nd edn, Wm. Blackwood & Sons (Edinburgh, 1840), pp. 55–56.

11 See the discussion in Chapter 9, 'Roslyn Chapel' *infra*.

12 Aitken, 'The Knights Templar in Scotland', p. 21.

13 Ibid., p. 15.

14 Cowan, Ian B., Mackay, P.H.R. & Macquarrie, Alan, *The Knights of St. John of Jerusalem In Scotland*, Scottish History Society (Edinburgh, 1983), p. xxiii.

15 Aitken, 'The Knights Templar in Scotland', p. 16.

16 Lord, Evelyn, *The Knights Templar in Britain*, Pearson Education Limited (Edinburgh, 2002), pp. 130, 131.

17 Ibid., p. 108.

18 Ibid., p. 65.

19 Aitken, 'The Knights Templar in Scotland', p. 9.

20 Edwards, 'The Knights Templar in Scotland', *Transactions*, p. 38.

21 Cowan, Mackay & Macquarrie, *The Knights of St. John of Jerusalem in Scotland*, pp. 41–42.

22 Edwards, 'The Knights Templar in Scotland', p. 39. The nature of the punishment is unknown.

23 Described in the following chapter.

24 See: Edwards, 'The Knights Templar in Scotland', p. 42, and Perkins, Clarence, 'The Knights Templars in the British Isles', *The English Historical Review* (April 1910), p. 222.

25 Cowan, Mackay & Macquarrie, *The Knights of St. John of Jerusalem in Scotland*, p. xxii.

26 Edwards, 'The Knights Templar in Scotland', *Transactions*.

27 Cowan, Mackay & Macquarrie, *The Knights of St. John of Jerusalem in Scotland*, p. 192.

28 Bartholomew could also have been the Master between 1260 and 1265.

29 Aitken, 'The Knights Templar in Scotland', p. 22.

30 Brian de Jay was later elevated to be the Master of England and lived at the Templar House in London.

31 The full story is set forth in a charter by Brother Thomas de Lindesay, Master of the Hospital of St John of Jerusalem, to Robert, Son of Alexander Wimple of Haukerstoun (the charter of 1354) at 'Blantordokis' [Balantrodoch], which is reproduced in an article by John Edwards, 'The Templars in Scotland in the Thirteenth Century', published in the

Scottish Historical Review, 1908. The article contains the charter transcribed in Latin and translated into English.

32 Aitken, 'The Knights Templar in Scotland', p. 24.

33 Balantrodoch was administered by William Slyeth, Bailiff; Adam Morcell, Sergeant; and Adam de Wedale, Forester. Others signing the charter of 1354 were Adam de Hermistoun, Thomas de Megeth, Alan de Yorkystoun, Adam de Wedeale, Alan de Wedale, John de Catkoyne, Alan son of Symon de Heriouth, Thomas son of Hugo de Middleton, and John Bell de Locworward.

34 Proceedings of the Society of the Antiquaries, 'Temple Midlothian' (1911–1912), p. 409.

35 Burnes, *Sketch of the History of the Knights Templar*, p. 56.

36 Mander, Bob, 'Balantrodoch: The Scottish Temple', in *The Templar Papers*, ed. Oddvar Olsen, New Page Books (Forest Lakes, 2006), p. 187.

37 *Fortean Times*, May 2001.

38 Mander, 'Balantrodoch', *The Templar Papers*, p. 179.

3

TEMPLAR LIFE, RIGHTS AND PRIVILEGES

A description and discussion of the Templars' properties in Scotland carries with it an understanding of the extent of the Templars in Scotland, who they were, and what they did. More often than not, when one sees something labeled 'Properties' one thinks of lists and a dull series of transactions describing who sold or leased what to whom. These do exist. But what is intriguing is the data and wealth of information they contain. The information is essential because there is a paucity of records about the Templars' activities, and there are no remnants of Templar buildings. But the property records tell much of the story of the Templars, who they were and what they did, from the time of their arrival in Scotland in 1129, until their inquisition in 1309.

Most books deal with the Templars from their initial creation in Jerusalem in 1119, to their abolition by Pope Clement V's papal bull *Vox in excelso* in 1312 at the Council of Vienna. Most of the studies of the Templars concentrate on their beginning, anecdotal accounts of their temples and houses throughout continental Europe and in England, their major battles, and the events leading up to and resulting in their arrest, torture, trial and dissolution. They do not deal with, or focus on Scotland.[1] They do not center on the Templars' daily lifestyle in Scotland, or note that the Knights Templar in Scotland were as much monks as those in Europe and Outremer. But from a review of the writings and documents that involve Templar properties, and the events and circumstances that surround them, there is enough to gain an understanding of the Scottish Knights Templar, and to learn that what may seem to have been myths and fantasies have a basis in fact.

THE PRECEPTORY OF MARYCULTER

Maryculter is the other of the two Templar preceptories in Scotland. It was second to Balantrodoch, but just as well known. Like Balantrodoch, it was a primary Templar residence where the knights lived, prayed and managed the Templar enterprises that ranged throughout Scotland. It was located on the south side of the lower River Dee, about eight miles west and to the south of Aberdeen. The land was originally granted to the Templars by King William I, 'the Lion' (1165–1214), who is famous for founding Arbroath Abbey in 1178. Ultimately, Maryculter grew to be in excess of 8,000 acres after Walter Byset donated a house and more land in 1239. In terms of development, it was begun in the late twelfth or early thirteenth century. It was completed around 1287. The principle source of revenue was from agriculture that was carried out by tenants who planted crops, raised sheep, harvested peat, and carried out woodcutting.

On the other side of the River Dee were Peterculter and Kelso Abbey. There was no bridge over the river between the Templars' preceptory and the abbey. This meant that the Templars did not have access to Kelso Abbey's church, which resulted in an arbitration that demonstrated the determination and influence of the Templars. The events leading up to and resulting from the arbitration are preserved in the episcopal chartulary of Aberdeen. The document provides an interesting glimpse of the Templars' relations with the ecclesiastical orders in Scotland, and the kinds of disputes caused by the Templars' extraordinary privileges. The parish church of Culter had jurisdiction over both sides of the Dee. It did not belong to the Templars, but to the monks of Kelso, who had obtained an indult from Pope Urban IV which stated that no one in any of their parishes should rebuild any church or chapel without their consent.

In spite of this, and because the abbey was on the other side of the river, the Templars built a chapel for themselves and their tenants on their side of the River Dee. They also refused to pay the tithes due from their lands. The monks at Kelso Abbey were unhappy because they saw the Templar chapel as a threat to their income. It was also a violation of the original grant. The monks therefore asked for both the payment of the tithes, and for the destruction of the chapel. The Templars refused, and in 1287 the monks commenced arbitration. The Templars replied by referring to their privileges, and claimed that the river was too wide and the chapel was necessary. They pointed out that they were exempt from paying tithes from wastelands which they had brought into cultivation. This included the lands of Estirtully, Kincolsy, and the two Deliburries, as well as those of Tulichezirt and Blairs, which had formerly been part of the royal forest. Further, in these wastelands they were privileged to erect churches with cemeteries for themselves, their vassals, and for way-farers. Because the parish church of Culter was on the north bank of the Dee, and, as the river had no bridge, their men, living on the south side, often could not get to Mass without danger. As a result, they had built the chapel, with cemetery and baptistery, at their house at Culter, and had possessed it peacefully, along with the tithes of their lands, for more than forty years.

The dispute was settled. The Templars were allowed to keep their chapel and teinds, but were required to pay compensation to the monks of Kelso of eight marks a year. Maryculter became a separate parish. The result of this dispute is evidenced today by the existence of the two parishes of Peterculter and Maryculter.

Maryculter was ultimately abandoned in 1548. When this occurred, there were only six knights and their chaplain remaining in the pre-ceptory. There were two Polwarts, two Widderburns, one Ducanson, one Ingles, and the chaplain, whose name was MacNicol.[2] Currently the chapel is in ruin, but the graveyard remains intact along the side of the River Dee.

TEMPLAR PROPERTIES AND TENANTS

The Templar enterprises involved hundreds of people. First, the records establish that there was a hierarchy. There were probably more than forty to fifty Templars in Scotland, in addition to the four knights who are known to have been there when two were arrested just before the inqui-sition.[3] The additional Templars were not all knights. Many were sergeants who managed the properties, maintained the preceptories, and accounted for the income from the numerous houses and lands. In addition, each shire or baillie had what was known as a bailli. A bailli was a Templar sergeant,[4] or an employee who acted as an overseer and collected rents for the area he commanded.[5] The bailli and his functions continued for several hundred years after the Templars were formally dissolved.

The Templars owned property in almost every area and shire in Scotland, and the bailli in the shire was responsible for managing approximately 517 properties.[6] The only Scottish sheriffdom where the Templars did not own land was Argyll.[7] Basically, the Templars' only real item of overhead was labor. The conditions under which the Templars held their properties were regarded as a model of the most favorable kind of tenure. This is demonstrated by a quote from a charter from William the Lion that granted lands to the Priory of St Andrews 'with the same freedom from all custom, service, and exaction as is everywhere enjoyed by the brethren of the Hospital and the Temple'.[8] These freedoms were also set forth in a charter from King Alexander II, which was taken from the text of a similar charter issued by Henry III of England. The Templars and their tenants were exempt from all courts other than Templar courts. They were also exempt from taxes, or from serving on juries. The tenants had the right to practice any trade they chose, and did not have to belong to one of the incorporated guilds or trade organizations.[9] Templars held their lands with all the common feudal rights. But they were free from all feudal aids, and exaction, whether for the king himself or his ministers. In addition, any lands that the Templars reclaimed and cultivated, even if they were within the bounds of the royal forest, were exempt from tithes and the forest laws.

The crops harvested on the Templar estates and properties were basic. They consisted of barley (which was known then as bere), oats, wheat, pease and hay. The primary source for wheat was the rich land at Liston, where bere was also grown. The source of meat was primarily from the various kinds of poultry, supplemented with beef and lamb. Perch, pike and eels were harvested from the lochs, with trout from the streams, and occasionally salmon. Also, the types of Templar holdings varied. With the tenement in Glasgow, the Templars owned nearby land that included fishing rights in the Firth of Clyde which realised a net profit that was sent to the Holy Land of twelve pence a year.[10]

Agriculture and fishing were the basic source of the Templars' income. But the Templars required more than just a share of the crops. Some tenants were required to do a certain number of days plowing in the winter, harrowing in Lent, and harvesting in the autumn. For this the tenant was fed meal and a pound of cheese at supper. Others were required to lend their horses to transport goods between Balantrodoch and other Templar lands such as Kirkliston or Maryculter. Of course, all the tenants in the area were thirled to the Templar mill. That is, they were bound to use the Templar mill to grind their grain, and to pay the going rate. Colts that were foaled on a tenant's land belonged to the Templars to increase their horse inventory. They also followed the feudal custom of requiring a bride to obtain a license from the Templars before marrying.[11] Each year, the tenant paid the Templars twelve pence at the feast of St Michael. He was entitled to all of the Order's royal and papal privileges and was not amenable to the local courts, and, as described earlier, he was not subject to the usual dues, tolls, exact or duties imposed upon the other tenants of local landowners.[12]

The smaller Templar properties, and portions of the larger ones, were worked by tenants. The farmer of Templar land had a continuing and consistent landlord. There was an element of certainty that did not exist on other farms where the farmer would dread a change of lord. The situation was aptly described by Alexander Walker in a paper he read at a meeting of the Aberdeen Philosophical Society in 1887. His remarks were directed to the tenants of the Knights Templar at Maryculter, but they applied to any of the Templar tenants:

> The farmer had a deathless landlord then, not a harsh guardian or a grinding mortgagee, or a dilatory Master in Chancery. All was certain. The manor had not to dread a change of lord, or the oaks to tremble at the axe of the squandering heir. The method is in startling contrast to that pursued in our day by many owners of land, who really seem to make their estates little better than agricultural workshops to raise money, forgetful of the heavy obligation they lie under to the country to raise and maintain a strong and hardy population, whose brawny arms may, when needed, defend the empire. The offspring of the workshop and the mill – weaklings of the city – can never do it.[13]

The differences between a Templar and common tenant led to irreconcilable and incongruous situations. Consider two neighbors: One was a Templar tenant and the other was the tenant of a poor landlord.

As shown above, the Templar tenant had a deathless landlord who was interested in the long-run continuity of income production, not short-term cash flow to finance his castle and lifestyle. When the Templar tenant took his crops to market, he did not have to wait in line and pay road tolls. He did not have to pay duties every time he crossed the lands and estates of different owners. The Templar tenant did not have to pay taxes and assessments to the county or the local town. They did not have to suffer the periodic indelicate conduct of tax collectors. The Templar tenant was only responsible to the Templar bailli. Tenants of the larger Templar estates dealt with sergeants. The guilds did not take the situation lightly. They were able to obtain some degree of protection from the Scottish Parliament with a decree that no Templar should meddle in buying or selling goods belonging to the guild unless the Templar was a guild member himself. But this probably had little impact on the Templars' power in the marketplace.

The sons of the Templar tenants had an unusual amount of career mobility because they did not have to join a guild. If a Templar tenant's son found that he had a talent for shoeing horses or making candles, he could become a smith or a chandler, free from the entry restrictions imposed by the guilds. And, if the son was very good at his trade, he did not have to worry about being driven out of business because he had the reputation of the Templars behind him. As a result, the Templar tenant's income may have been comparable to that of the other tenants, but his and his family's lifestyle was enviable.

With all their property and estates, the net revenue the Templars sent to the Holy Land from Scotland was relatively small. At the end of the twelfth century, the Templar estates generated about 300 marks per year. The rate was about 1.74 pounds to the mark or £170. In 1890 this equaled £2,400.[14] In 2007, this amount would have a buying power of £62,400. But the Templars in Scotland utilized very effective management practices and, during the next hundred years, the annual income from the Templar lands tripled. At the end of the thirteenth century the Master in Scotland paid a remittance to Outremer of about 900 marks per year, or £515, which calculates to a current value of £189,000. This was about one-third of what was being earned in England, where the annual remittance to Outremer was about 3,000 marks per year. Remittances from Scotland continued until the Scottish War of Independence broke out with the Battle of Stirling Bridge in

1297. Then the remittances ceased, and nothing further was sent from Scotland to London.[15]

TEMPLAR PROPERTIES

Today there are at least forty-eight sites that can be identified as being originally involved with the Templars.[16] While James Maidment lists over 500 Templar properties, most authors discuss only a few. The three that have been most frequently described are:

1. Balantrodoch, the principal Templar preceptory and residence of the Templar Master in Scotland.
2. Maryculter in Kincardineshire, the second preceptory, which is discussed later in this chapter.
3. Temple Liston, located in West-Lothian on the Almond River in Linlithgowshire. It is the older name for what is now Kirkliston. The property was granted to the Templars in the twelfth century. Currently the town is known for its fine Norman church that has no relation to the Templars. The Templars are known to have had a temple in Liston. Unfortunately nothing of it remains.

Aboyne in Aberdeenshire is a church that is about thirty miles up the River Dee from Maryculter, on land given to the Templars by Walter Byset. It was granted by Ralph, Bishop of Aberdeen *ad propier usus* in around 1242. By the terms of the grant the Templars were obligated to maintain a vicar in the church, and to present him, duly qualified, to the bishop, to whom he was answerable 'in spiritual matters and for the cure of souls'.[17] This grant was confirmed by Pope Alexander IV in a papal bull. And, there is actual evidence of this record by the presentation of a certain John of Annan, King's Chaplain, to be vicar of Aboyne in 1277.

Ayrshire in south-west Scotland was one of the most significant locations. The Templars did not have a preceptory in Ayrshire, but they did own a significant number of houses and farms. This is evident by the number of current Templar addresses in Ayrshire.[18] It is believed that because of the extent of the Templar holdings in Ayrshire, the Templar fleet that left France in 1307 and sailed for Scotland did not land here but proceeded on to Argyll.

With over 500 properties, there were hundreds of tenants. In Fifeshire alone there were at least thirty-five farms or tenements.[19] There was not a royal burgh in which the Templars did not own two or more houses. The best examples were found in Edinburgh and St Andrews. In Edinburgh, the areas of Grassmarket and West Bow were Templar lands. The Templars had at least twelve houses or tenements in the St Andrews area. In Cupar, there were two with gardens running down to the Eden, and there were several Templar houses in Aberdeen. Strathmiglo had two or three; Dunfermline possessed two; Kinghorn also had two or three; and Inverkeiting had several. The Templars' selection of houses was said to be very judicious, and they were well cared for, many with gardens to the rear.[20]

Other sites that have been identified and for which there is little or no description are:

Aggerstone in Stirlingshire;
Derville or Derval in Ayrshire;
Dinwoodie in Dumfriesshire;
Inchynan was a parish church in Renfrewshire;
Kingcausie near Aberdeen;
Red-abbey-stedd in Roxburghshire;
Tullich near Aberdeen;
Turriff near Aberdeen;
The land and salt pits at Falkirk;
Land at the great and wealthy seaport of Berwick.

East Fenton, Peffer, Swanston, Callander Saltworks, and Guillane are listed by Evelyn Lord in *The Knights Templar in Britain*, but are not discussed.[21]

Due to the similarity of its name, Culter in Lanarkshire is a house that is often confused with Maryculter. It has no connection. Apparently it was a house owned by the Templars and leased to a tenant. It was not a 'Templar house' in the context of a preceptory such as Balantrodoch or Maryculter.

Currently, the focal point for many of today's Scottish Templar Knights is Balgonie Castle, a location that may be the only site in Scotland that has significance for Scotland's first Templars and those of today.

Construction of Balgonie Castle is believed to have begun in the fourteenth century on the south bank of the River Leven, which flows from Loch Leven (where Mary Queen of Scots was imprisoned) to the

Firth of Forth just south of the town of Markinch. The first recorded lairds of Balgonie were the Sibbald family who held the office of Constable of Cupar in 1120. Their probable connection to the Templars is demonstrated by their arms, which are almost identical to the Temple arms with a red cross on a white background. The only difference is the square hole in the center of the cross.

The significance of the area is demonstrated by the fact that there are also many sites around Balgonie that have Temple in their name, indicating that they had once belonged to the Order. In addition, a Valuation Roll of 1539 lists a site called 'Temple of Balgonie'. Unfortunately, the site has not yet been identified.

Today, the laird of Balgonie is Raymond Morris of Balgonie and Eddergoll, who is the Grand Prior of the Grand Priory of the Scots. He is also an honorary member in the Autonomous Grand Priory of Scotland. Balgonie Castle hosts investitures for not only the Grand Priory of the Scots, but the Autonomous Grand Priory of Scotland, the Grand Priory of Scotland and the OSMTH.

DISSOLUTION

In 1312, when the Templars were formally dissolved, Pope Clement V's papal bull *Adprovidam* transferred the Templars' lands and holdings to the Hospitallers. But this did not happen quickly. In England, the Hospitallers did not obtain title to any Templar properties for twelve years after the Pope's order. In Scotland there is no record of an actual transfer. The closest thing are letters from King Edward I to his Scottish chancellor, Albert de Nigro Castro, and chamberlain, Leonard de Tibercis, ordering that all of the churches, houses, manors, land and rents of the Templars in Scotland, together with the crops in their fields and ornaments of their churches, be delivered to two commissioners appointed by the Grand Master of the Order of St John of Jerusalem. There is a record of their traveling to Scotland, but there is no record of their doing anything to enforce the order when they arrived.[22]

While there is no record of actual transfers, there is proof that the Hospitallers did not receive any of the Temple lands until after 1338. But by 1354 the Hospitallers were in possession of Balantrodoch, and their own knights and administrators were managing it.[23] But the remaining

Templar properties were catalogued and managed separately. Normally, new properties are immediately incorporated into an existing inventory, but this did not happen with the Templar estates, houses and properties.[24] They were not only listed separately, but the properties were managed separately. Each shire continued to have its Temple bailli who was the property manager and collected rents in each area.[25] This practice continued for over 200 years and was adopted by the Hospitallers, but not fully implemented into their administrative practices until the late fifteenth century.[26]

During this time, the separate existence of the Templars was acknowledged by King James IV. The Register of the Great Seal of Scotland contains a document dated 1488 by James IV confirming all former grants of land made to '*Sancto Hospitali de Jerusalem, et fratribus ejusdem militia Templi Salomonis*'.[27] This reference to the Templars is said to prove that the Templar Order maintained an existence that was united with the Hospitallers.[28] And it may well be that the Order did continue to exist in some form. The charter of James IV refers to two previous confirmations – one dated at Stirling on 7 May 1448, and one on 20 February 1482. Neither of these documents refers to the suppression of the Templars; 'not one word from the beginning to the end occurs indicative of such an occurrence'.[29] The importance of this omission is highlighted by the fact that the Hospitallers' Preceptor of Torphichen was William Knollis, and that William Knollis was King James IV's treasurer and a confidante of the king. In this situation, there is little doubt that William Knollis played a part in the drafting of the charter, and that he would certainly have included something in it to remove any doubt that the Templars had been dissolved and were no longer involved. But he didn't. It is an omission that speaks loudly.

Until 1528 the Templar houses and lands remained under the umbrella of the Hospitallers' Order of St John of Jerusalem. But in 1528, the Scottish Parliament of James V passed an Act authorizing 'religious corporations' to sell their lands to 'substantial men' who could improve them.[30] The first sale under this Act happened in 1535, when the portion of Maryculter known as Kingcausie was sold to Harry, third son of the laird of Drum. This was the first transfer of one of the properties that had been accumulated by the Knights Templar.[31] Before this, up to 517 properties had been held as a unit listed by the Hospitallers as 'Terrae Templariae', a self-contained and separately administered Templar patrimony![32]

Sales continued for the next ten to fifteen years. Portions of Maryculter continued to be sold. In July of 1535 Gilbert Menzies, laird of Findon obtained what is now the estate of Blairs, belonging to the college of that name. A few years later, all the parts of Maryculter lying to the west of Kingcausie were acquired by the laird of Petfodels. This portion consisted of about 5,000 acres and ultimately became the estates of Maryculter and Ashentilly.

The Hospitallers' ownership of their own and the Templar property came to an end on 22 January 1563 when James Sandelands, the Master of the Order of St John, relinquished the estates, houses and lands of the Hospitallers and the Templars to Queen Mary of Scotland. Specifically, he transferred the estates and houses at Torphichen, Tankertoun, Dennie, Balantrodoch, Maryculter, Temple Liston, Inchynan, Aboyne, Stanhope, and Galtua. He did this together 'with their pertinents, lying in the Sheriffdoms, of Edinburgh, Pebles, Lilithgow, Striueling, Lanerk Kincardin and Stewartry of Kirkcudbritht, and also of all annual rents, templar lands, teinds, possessions and lands whatsoever as well not named as named within the Kingdom of Scotland'.[33] But with this transfer came another small piece of evidence of the Templars' continued existence. Among the Sandilands' family documents is a description of the transactions.[34] This description contains the statement that the properties were 'never subject to any Chapter or Conuent whatsomever, except only the Knights of Jerusalem [Hospitallers] and the Temple of Solomon [Templars]'.

With this transfer, the holding of the Templars as a corporation came to an end. But it was not the end of the Templar influence. The privileges that existed before 1307 were carried on, attached to, and stayed with the land. Until 1563, owners and tenants were exempt from all courts except Torphichen. Until 1748, owners of Templar property were exempt from taxes, or serving on juries, and they had the right to practice any trade they chose and did not have to belong to one of the incorporated guilds or trade organizations.

The Templars' churches, churchyards and chapels, along with those of the Hospitallers, continued to possess the right of girth, or sanctuary. King Alexander II had granted the Scottish Templars a comprehensive charter that formally recognized their right of sanctuary as applying to murder, robbery, and other crimes of violence. Considering the amount of abuse that was charged against the Templars in the latter part of the thirteenth century and in 1307, it is surprising that there were no complaints about any alleged abuses of this privilege. But then, what murderer or robber would want to seek sanctuary in a Templar church, and be subject to the discipline of knights who could easily enforce their way of life on the miscreant who sought their help? But the tradition was well known and did not die with the formal abolition of the Templars. It continued well into the mid-1700s. In the county of Fifeshire alone, these privileges applied to thirty-five Templar and twelve Hospitaller properties.[35] The situation is amusingly illustrated in the story of a woman who incurred the displeasure of the town's officials. She took refuge in a Templar tenement, and then defied the town officers to arrest 'or lay hands upon her'.[36]

> Some few years since, an old woman who had got into a squabble with the civic dignitaries of [the town of] Kinghorn, and was under their ban, rushed from the presence-chamber, pursued by the town officer, and darting into a temple Tenement, ascended one flight of stairs, and looking over a window, shook her fist at her pursuer and bade him defiance. Whether impressed with a belief of the right of sanctuary, or frightened by the virago's hostile demeanour, we know not, but true it is and of verity that the man stopped his pursuit, and left the honour of victory with his antagonist.[37]

But there was also an economic side to the situation. This is illustrated in the case of *Ross of Auchlossin against the Possessors of Temple-Lands*.[38] The opinion does not set forth the facts, but it is apparent that Ross of Auchlossin was not receiving rent from the tenants of the lands that he owned that were originally owned by the Templars. The issue was clear: were the lands ecclesiastical or secular? If they were ecclesiastic, they were annexed to the Crown and no rent was paid to Ross of Auchlossin. But if they were secular, the lands were not annexed and Ross of Auchlossin could enforce his right to receive rent.

The opinion goes into a substantial amount of historical detail about the Templars, beginning with their creation to assist travelers in 1118 through their arrest and dissolution. Ultimately, it is held that the Templars, after their arrest, were secular, but of more importance, it was held that the Templar revenues were never ecclesiastical.

The case also illustrates how slowly things changed and the strength of the Templar influence. Consider – the case arose 394 years after the dissolution of the Templars.

TEMPLAR PROPERTIES TODAY

Currently everything that the Templars owned was either sold or is now a public place or street. Balantrodoch is now the remains of a church in the town of Temple. Maryculter has a new church, but the cemetery remains. By and large, all that is left is names. But Templar names and places abound in Scotland, and are being compiled by the Rosslyn Templars. Currently its list contains eighty-nine sites. They are listed on its website, www.rosslyntemplars.org.uk/scotland.htm, together with the applicable postcodes. From there, one can view the relevant street map of the location and zoom towards the site.

From what little records do exist, we know that there were substantially more than four men to run all of the Templars' holdings. There was a hierarchy and infrastructure with a central command. It remained intact, without interference by the Hospitallers, for over twenty years after the formal dissolution of the Templars. It was a framework into which escaped Templars could blend. There was no need for secret preceptories in the outer isles. The circumstances lead to the conclusion that the Templars' infrastructure in Scotland was soon separated from control by the Master at the Temple in London. If this were the case, then for at least twenty years after the arrest of the Templars, the existing preceptories could welcome those Templars who chose to come to Scotland. There is no need to rely on the fantasies that Stephen Howarth describes as having been born centuries after the Order's suppression. There are numerous facts upon which one can base a foundation for the continued existence of the Templars.

NOTES

1   Two exceptions are found in parts of Baigent and Leigh, *The Temple and the Lodge*, Arcade Publishing (New York, 1989), and Lord, Evelyn, *The Knights Templar in Britain*, Pearson Education Limited (Edinburgh, 2002).

2   Walker, Alexander, 'The Knights Templar In & Around Aberdeen', *The Aberdeen Journal*, Aberdeen University Press (16 March 1887), pp. 14–15.

3   Aitken, Robert, 'The Knights Templar in Scotland', *The Scottish Review* (July 1898), p. 14, citing Addison's *Knights Templar* (2nd edn), pp. 103, 467.

4   Upton-Ward, J.M., *The Rule of the Templars*, The Boydell Press (Suffolk, 1992), p. 30.

5 Baigent and Leigh, *The Temple and the Lodge*, p. 275.
6 Ibid. This fact is extrapolated from the *Abstract of the Charters and other papers recorded in the Chartulary of Torphichen from 1581 to 1596*, ed. James Maidment (Edinburgh, 1830), who catalogued the Templar properties held by the Order of St John after the dissolution of the Templars.
7 Aitken, 'The Knights Templar in Scotland', p. 10.
8 Ibid., p. 9.
9 Leighton, John M., *History of the County of Fife*, vol. 3, Appendix A, 'Historical Account of the Knights Templar and their Possessions in Fife', Joseph Swan (Glasgow, 1840), p. 258.
10 Aitken, 'The Knights Templar in Scotland', p. 11.
11 Ibid., p. 20.
12 Edwards, John, 'The Knights Templar in Scotland', *Transactions of the Scottish Ecclesiological Society*, Vol. IV (Aberdeen, 1912–1915), p. 39.
13 Walker, 'The Knights Templar In & Around Aberdeen', *The Aberdeen Journal*, pp. 20–21.
14 Coutts, Rev. Alfred, *The Knights Templar in Scotland* (Edinburgh, 1890), p. 12.
15 Edwards, 'The Knights Templar in Scotland', *Transactions*, p. 38.
16 Rosslyn Templars, www.rosslyntemplars.org.uk/
17 Aitken, 'The Knights Templar in Scotland', p. 12.
18 www.rosslyntemplars.org.uk/scotland.htm
19 Leighton, John M., *History of the County of Fife*, pp. 256-257.
20 Ibid., p. 258.
21 Lord, *The Knights Templar in Britain*, p. 143.
22 Aitken, 'The Knights Templar in Scotland', p. 35.
23 Edwards, 'The Knights Templar in Scotland', *Transactions*, p. 46.
24 It could be that the Hospitallers did not create a new record and make the existing one redundant. This could be true were it not for the cadre of Templar baillis that were in place.
25 Baigent & Leigh, *The Temple and the Lodge*, p. 275.
26 Cowan, Ian B., Mackay, P.H.R. & Macquarrie, Alan, *The Knights of St. John of Jerusalem In Scotland*, Scottish History Society (Edinburgh, 1983), p. lxviii.
27 Cooper, Robert L.D., *The Rosslyn Hoax? Viewing Rosslyn Chapel from a new perspective*, Lewis (UK, 2006), p. 235.
28 Leighton, *History of the County of Fife*, p. 254. But in *The Rosslyn Hoax?* the author claims that this interpretation is wrong. In making this assertion, however, the author overlooks the fact that the Templar properties in Scotland were not transferred to the Hospitallers until after 1338, or that

the Templars had in place baillis whose successors continued to manage the holdings until 1563.

29 Leighton, *History of the County of Fife*, p. 254.

30 Walker, 'The Knights Templars In & Around Aberdeen', *The Aberdeen Journal*, p. 14.

31 Ibid.

32 Baigent & Leigh, *The Temple and the Lodge*, p. 97.

33 National Archives of Scotland, document GD19/34.

34 'Templaria' (Edinburgh, 1825); Burnes, *History of the Knights Templar*, p. 65.

35 Leighton, *History of the County of Fife*, pp. 256–257.

36 *Abstract of the Chartulary of Torphichen*, Introduction, p. 3, cited in Robert Aitken, 'The Knights Templar in Scotland', p. 9.

37 Leighton, *History of the County of Fife*, p. 259.

38 Information, *Ross of Auchlossin against the Possessors of Temple-Lands* (Edinburgh, 1706), National Library of Scotland. The facts stated in the Information are surprisingly consistent with those that are known and frequently written about today. It is interesting to read that the thought processes of the triers of fact in the early eighteenth century are not unlike those of today's judges. The Information starts out reciting the facts in favor of the Possessers of Templar-Lands, which are stronger than those of Ross of Auchlossin, and then proceeds to find every fact possible to support a decision for Ross. Among today's lawyers, it is called the doctrine of 'the right result'.

4

THE EXCOMMUNICATION
OF ROBERT THE BRUCE

From the facts and circumstances that surround the Battle of Bannockburn, it is evident that the Templars were there. Their motivations for being present were rooted in 1292 when King Edward I selected John Balliol to be King of Scotland. But the single most important event happened fourteen years later in 1306, eight years before the Battle of Bannockburn at the site of what is now Greyfriars Church in Dumfries. That event was a significant and historic application of the 'law of unintended consequences'.

In 1306, before the Battle of Bannockburn, the King of Scotland owed fealty to the King of England, Edward I. As a result, Scotland was not truly independent, and its king had to be acceptable to England's king.

The events leading up to the excommunication of Robert the Bruce began in about 1290 when Scotland's throne was vacant. There were many contenders for the throne, but only two had a real claim. One was John Balliol, Lord of Galloway. He was not only a direct descendant of David I, but he had the support of the Comyn family because his sister had married a Comyn. The other was Robert I, Lord of Annandale, also known as Robert the Competitor, the grandfather of Robert the Bruce. To settle the matter, King Edward opened a great court in June 1291. Each of the contenders then submitted a petition that contained a detailed provenance and the reasons why he should be crowned.[1] The petitions were received and the great court was continued until June 1292. Apparently the members of the great court wanted to delay making a decision because it was again continued to 14 October 1292. Then, with more than a little nudging from King Edward, on 17 November 1292 the great court named John Balliol the heir at law to the Scottish throne.

John Balliol was crowned King of Scotland, but he was never in any real sense a king. He was constantly humiliated by King Edward who had given himself the title of overlord of Scotland.[2] He was not recognized as king by many Scots, including Robert I, who would never tender homage or fealty to John Balliol. As a result, Balliol abdicated on 10 July 1296. For the next ten years the throne remained vacant. Two major contenders emerged: Robert the Bruce, the grandson of Robert I, and John 'The Red' Comyn. The Comyn family's roots were English. John's was the more direct line, and he had the backing of King Edward. Robert the Bruce's family stemmed from the de Brus line in France, and he was said to be from the noblest stock in all England.[3] As a result, two powerful leaders were in direct conflict for the Scottish throne.

The excommunication of Robert the Bruce stems from the fact that he stabbed John Comyn in front of the altar of the Monastery of the Grey Friars. This fact is well known and well documented. But the facts leading up to the stabbing of John Comyn are not.

The best known version begins in 1205 when King Edward became extremely ill; many believed him to be near death. To Robert the Bruce, this seemed a good opportunity to negotiate a compromise that would avoid a direct conflict with John Comyn. Robert the Bruce made an imaginative proposal: he would cede his lands to Comyn if Comyn would back him as King of Scotland. Or, in the alternative, Comyn would cede his lands to Bruce and Bruce would back Comyn for the throne. Comyn agreed, and they each signed and sealed the agreement which also contained a bond of secrecy.[4] John Comyn chose to have the land and, ostensibly, pledged his support for Robert the Bruce. But no sooner had John Comyn made his agreement than he gave King Edward a copy of Bruce's indenture. Edward, who had recovered from his illness, was furious.

But these narratives are not without controversy. A historian writing in 1797 notes that when this agreement was supposedly made, Bruce stood in high favor with King Edward; that he was consulted and trusted. Accordingly, such a proposal, made in such circumstances, would naturally have alarmed the suspicions of Comyn and would have made him 'apprehend a *false confidense*'. The historian also points out something that upon reflection appears obvious:

> It must be held extraordinary, that the two conspirators, met together, should have committed such a secret to writing, as if it had been a legal covenant to have force in a court of justice; but more extraordinary still, that they should have done this at the imminent hazard of intrusting their lives and fortunes to the fidelity of a third party, for, I presume, it will be admitted, that two Scottish barons, in that age, could not have formed such an indenture without assistance.[5]

There are two versions of what happened next.

One holds that when King Edward was shown the indenture he was enraged. To gain Bruce's presence in London, he called a session of Parliament. Bruce arrived in late January or early February and was called to a meeting with King Edward. The king was very abrupt, and the meeting did not go well. When Bruce left the meeting he had no idea why the king was so angry. But nothing further occurred and a short time later Bruce was on his way back to Scotland. On his way, he intercepted a courier for John Comyn. The courier was, unfortunately, carrying a message from Comyn to the king which confirmed Comyn's disclosure of their agreement. Robert the Bruce's immediate reaction was to relieve the poor courier of his head. Bruce then arranged the meeting with John Comyn in the church at the Abbey of the Franciscans, who were known as the Grey Friars. But this version is not without problems. Apparently, it is easily established that Parliament was not in session. In addition, Comyn's messenger was on foot and had to travel 400 miles in the month of February after a snowstorm and a severe frost.[6]

The other version is that upon learning of the indenture that had been agreed between Robert the Bruce and John Comyn, the king immediately summoned Bruce to London to appear before the privy council.[7] They met on 2 February 1306. When King Edward handed Bruce the indenture with its seal, Bruce made a very adroit move. He informed the king that the indenture could not be his because he did not have possession of his seal. He then pledged to produce the true indenture, properly sealed, the next morning. But this was a ruse; Bruce's seal was with his clerk, and his clerk was staying with him at the inn.

When Bruce arrived back at the inn, he had two horses brought to him, and he and the clerk rode directly to Lochmaben. At the same time, John Comyn happened to be nearby, and agreed to meet with Bruce at the Monastery of the Grey Friars.[8]

Historians have also recited various versions of the events between Robert the Bruce and John Comyn inside the church. But each version is a good story on its own. And they all end with the same significant fact, that Robert the Bruce stabbed John Comyn in front of the altar at the Monastery of the Grey Friars.

It has been said that Bruce's murder of John Comyn was premeditated. But this does not fit with some of the circumstances. If Robert the Bruce had been courting John Comyn for support, why would he not continue to do this if he needed John's backing to win the crown? The Comyn family was one of the most powerful in Scotland. To incur its wrath would have been unwise. To commit the murder of another Scottish noble in a sacred church was a sacrilege. Likewise, if John Comyn was courting the support of Robert the Bruce and had proposed the exchange of lands and crown, as has also been suggested,[9] would Comyn go to such elaborate lengths to discredit Bruce after an agreement had been reached?

The Bruce family claimed that Robert the Bruce was at the Grey Friars Monastery to invoke Comyn's cooperation, and that Comyn provoked the attack.[10] This is consistent with the version told by Sir Herbert Maxwell, who believes that the offer for Bruce's lands or the Crown was made at the Monastery of the Grey Friars.[11]

Others describe an argument between them at the church as being between two hot-tempered men that ended when each drew his dagger, and Robert the Bruce inflicting the first and ultimately fatal wound.

From the chronology of events, it would seem likely that when Bruce learned of Comyn's betrayal, his reaction would be to seek retribution. If Bruce was to be charged with treason by King Edward, and if Bruce had returned to face the king the day after their meeting on 2 February 1306, Bruce's fate would undoubtedly have been execution, or imprisonment in the dungeon, and not the tower. His goal of becoming King of Scotland would have been unobtainable, and Comyn would have been crowned king by default. The only alternative was to remove John Comyn as a competitor.

Regardless of the motive or sequence of events, the result was that after he stabbed John Comyn, Robert the Bruce came rushing out of the church saying, 'For I doubt I have slain the Comyn'. Upon hearing this, Roger of Kirkpatrick said, 'I Mak Siccar' (I make certain), and rushed back into the church and stabbed Comyn again which ensured that John *The Red* Comyn was dead. The event is preserved on a plaque at the spot where it happened, which reads:

> Here stood the monastery
> of the GREY FRIARS where
> On Thursday 10th February
> 1306 ROBERT THE BRUCE
> aided by
> SIR ROGER KIRKPATRICK
> Slew THE RED COMYN AND
> Opened the final stage
> of the war for
> SCCOTTISH INDEPENDENCE
> Which ended victoriously on
> the FIELD of BANNOCKBURN
> 1314
> 'I Mak Siccar'

Several significant events followed:

On 25 March 1306 Robert the Bruce was crowned King of Scotland at the Abbey of Scone. Even though Scotland was in the middle of a frost, Robert the Bruce was not meant to be left in the cold. During his coronation he was warmed with the Scottish monarch's royal robes and vestments that the Bishop Wishart had hidden in his treasury. He was crowned with a circlet of gold. The coronation was attended by three bishops; among them was William Lamberton, Bishop of St Andrews. Two days later, Robert the Bruce was again crowned by Isabel, the sister of the Earl of Fife, who, by tradition, was responsible for placing the crown on each new Scottish king.[12] Because it was Palm Sunday, a Mass was celebrated and presided over by the same William Lamberton, Bishop of St Andrews.

When King Edward received word of the death of Comyn and the coronation of Bruce, he was furious. But there was little he could do. He could not capture and imprison Bruce, who was over 400 miles away and had a significant amount of popular support to the north and west of Edinburgh. And even though he was crowned King of Scotland, King Edward controlled most of Scotland and Bruce had no kingdom that could be attacked. But there was one thing King Edward could do. On 5 June 1306 he asked the Archdeacon of Middlesex, who was at St Paul's Cathedral, to excommunicate Robert the Bruce; which he did, along with Sir Roger of Kirkpatrick and James of Lindsey.[13] The archdeacon specifically declared that Robert the Bruce was no longer a son of the church.[14] The excommunication was ratified by Pope Clement V, who also placed an interdict on Scotland. This meant that the whole of Scotland was subject to excommunication, which created a significant schism between the Church in Rome and the Scottish clergy, who placed their allegiance with Bruce and Scotland, rather than with the Pope. The Scottish Church supported Robert the Bruce; the Church of Rome supported England and King Edward. As a result there was a clear line between them. The Scottish churchmen flatly refused to recognize the excommunication of their king, even after Bruce's excommunication was confirmed by Pope Clement V.[15] Bruce continued to worship in any parish he chose. The abbeys in Scotland welcomed and supported him.

The excommunication was not lifted until shortly before Bruce's death. And, because Clement V's successor, Pope John XXII, was also closely aligned with King Edward, he refused to acknowledge Robert the Bruce as the King of Scotland. Scotland was therefore unable to join the comity of nations.[16]

This all provided a receptive setting for the Knights Templar. They were disowned by the Pope, to whom the Templars originally owed their fealty, and who was initially their head. They were warrior-monks who naturally gravitated towards a receptive clergy. The Scottish clergy's allegiance was to Scotland, rather than the Pope. Scotland and her king were excommunicated. Where else could the Templars flee with impunity?

Little did King Edward I realize that his role in the excommunication of Robert the Bruce would be a significant factor in his son Edward II's defeat and humiliation eight years later at the Battle of Bannockburn. And in the interim there was the inquisition of the Knights Templar in Scotland, carried out two years later by none other than William Lamberton, Bishop of St Andrews. In this regard, there is also speculation that he was the facilitator of a secret agreement between Robert the Bruce and the Knights Templar who had fled the inquisition in England and the European continent.[17]

NOTES

1 Scott, Ronald McNair, *Robert the Bruce, King of Scots*, Carroll & Graf Publishers (New York, 1996), p. 27.

2 Ibid., p. 26.

3 Ibid., p. 28.

4 Barbour, Master John, *The Brus*, compiled 1375, translated by George Eyre-Todd, Gowans & Gray Limited (Glasgow, 1907), p. 13.

5 Dalrymple, Sir David, *Annals of Scotland*, Appendix No.VII, William Creech (Edinburgh, 1797), p. 49.

6 Ibid., p. 50. Sir David's critiques also illustrate what can be lost in translation. Regarding King Edward's calling a session of Parliament, Sir David recites, 'That Edward, having received Comyn's part of the indenture, summoned a Parliament, and that Bruce appeared *there:* That, on the first day of the Parliament, Edward exhibited the indenture, and charged Bruce as guilty of treason: that Bruce desired to have inspection of the indenture till next day, and pledged his whole estates for his appearance.'

7 Some versions of this story have Bruce coming to London to sit in Parliament as in the first version.

8 Barbour, *The Brus*, pp. 6–18.

9 Dalrymple, *Annals of Scotland*, p. 49.

10 Baker, Nina Brown, *Robert Bruce: King of Scots*, Vanguard Press (New York 1948), p. 59.

11 Maxwell, Sir Herbert, Bart. M.P., *Robert the Bruce and the Struggle for Scottish Independence*, 2nd edn, G.P. Putnam & Son, The Knickerbocker Press (New York, 1897), pp. 129–130.

12 Scott, *Robert the Bruce*, p. 76.

13 Maxwell, *Robert the Bruce*, p. 134.

14 Baker, *Robert the Bruce*, p. 136.

15 Ibid., p. 51.

16 Magnusson, Magnus, *Scotland: The Story of a Nation*, Atlantic Monthly Press (New York, 2000), p. 187.

17 There are many who believe the agreement between Bruce, Lamberton and the Templars to be a fact. See McKerrarcher, Archie, 'Bruce's Secret Weapon', *The Scots Magazine* (June 1991), p. 268. Mr McKerracher's arguments have been repeated in numerous publications.

5

THE TEMPLARS' ARRESTS

The premise that some of the Knights Templar fled to Scotland before and during the arrests is a simple one. But to fully understand and accept it, one must be familiar with the circumstances that led up to, and surrounded, the arrests of the Templars on Friday 13 October 1307.

The first significant event occurred on 14 September, when King Philip IV signed the order for the preparation of the arrest warrants for the Knights Templar, and the confiscation of their property. Matters concluded a month later.

THE PRINCIPAL PLAYERS

Obviously there were hundreds of people involved when the Templars were arrested. But only a few actively participated in the major events and are known. The ones whose roles are known to be significant are:[1]

Jacques de Molay – Grand Master of the Knights Templar from 1293 until his execution by King Philip IV on 18 March 1314.

Philip IV (known as *Le Bel* or Philip the Fair) – King of France from 1285 until his death on 29 November 1314.

Pope Clement V – Pope from 14 November 1305 until his death on 20 April 1314. He was considered to be a puppet of King Philip IV. Rather than being a puppet, Pope Clement V had health problems and was not politically adroit.

Hugh de Pairaud/Pérraud – Treasurer of the Temple. He held the office of Visitor General and was second only to de Molay.[2]

Gerard de Villiers – Preceptor of the Temple of France.

Hugh de Châlons – A knight and the nephew of Hugh de Pairaud.

Pierre Flote – Keeper of the Seals, and head of the Chandlery (candle makers and storage) from the early 1290s until his death in 1302.

Guillaume de Nogaret – A lawyer who was very influential from the mid-1290s. He became Keeper of the Seals from 1307 and held this position until his death in 1313.

THE CIRCUMSTANCES BEFORE THE ARRESTS

The Templars, Pope Clement V, and King Philip IV each had their own goals and agendas. To begin to understand the situation in 1307, one must go back to 1265 and the fall of the town of Caesarea and the fortress of Arsuf in Syria. With these, and a number of other defeats, the ultimate downfall of the Christians in Outremer was inevitable. During this period, the Templars went from the universal acceptance they enjoyed after the Council of Troyes, to alienation and distrust arising from their haughty and insular attitude, and their greed which emanated from their aggressive business practices. With the shrinking of the crusader states, there was also a waning interest among the Church and the nobility in Europe. In France, King Philip was more interested in expanding his kingdom. In England, Edward I had his hands full with the Scots. This left the crusades to the Pope and the Orders of the Templars, the Hospitallers, and the Teutonic Knights.

The problems accelerated after the fall of the city and Templar stronghold of Acre on 25 May 1291. After this, the original purpose of the

Knights Templar and the other Orders was gone. The Templars' role shifted from that of warrior to being managers of their estates, mills, wineries, tenants, livestock, and their treasury and banks. The rationale for their continued existence was the prospect of the Pope's authorization of another crusade at some point in the future. This required not only the management of the Templars' wealth, but its continued accumulation. Unfortunately, the Templars were primarily made up of poor knights or second sons who were illiterate, or barely literate, and who had not been trained in the use of power and authority. This resulted in an immense abuse of the Templars' power that had been consolidated by the numerous papal bulls and had given them immunity from local and secular authority. The consequence was an attitude of arrogance and greed. This is highlighted in the story that was told over 100 years ago.

In Sir John Mandeville's Travels a little anecdote is introduced graphically illustrating the aggrandizing spirit of the Order, and its fatal results. The author says: 'And in that country [Little Armenia] is an old castle that stands upon a rock, the which is clept the Castle of the Sparrow-hawk that is beyond the city of Layays [Lajazzo] beside the town of Pharsipee [Perschembé] that belongeth to the lordship of Cruck [Korgo] that is a rich lord and a good Christian man, where men find a sparrow-hawk upon a perch right fair and right well made, and a fair lady of faerie that keepeth it: And who that will watch the sparrow-hawk seven days and seven nights, and as some men say three days and three nights, without company and without sleep, that fair lady shall give him, when he hath done, the first wish that he will wish of earthly things; and that hath been proved oftentimes ... A Knight of the Temple watched there, and wished a purse evermore full of gold: And the lady granted him: But she said to him that he had asked the destruction of their Order, for the trust of the affiance of that purse, and for the great pride that they should have: And so it was.'[3]

Jacques de Molay became Grand Master in late 1293. His goals were to re-establish Christian authority in Outremer, and to preserve the integrity of the Order. As to the former, he continued to gather supplies in Italy and France, and to maintain a base on the small island of Ruad off the city of Tortosa in Syria. Unfortunately, when the base on Ruad was wiped out by a large Egyptian force in 1302, the Templars were forced off the island, and no longer had a stronghold in the Mediterranean east of Cyprus.

Between 1296 and 1306 the Templars were sometimes major participants in King Philip's financial affairs, and at other times they were rejected and ignored. But they were always, to varying degrees, his bankers. For example, between 1292 and 1295 King Philip moved much of his treasury to the Louvre, and out of Templar control. Then, after his defeat at Courtrai in 1302, he moved much of it back to the Templars' Paris Temple and ordered Hugh de Pairaud to collect war subsidies to cover the costs.

During the period that included the arrest and trials of the Templars, Pope Clement V's primary goal was to initiate another great crusade. This was probably done at the request of Philip IV who was always in need of revenue. To begin the process, in June 1306, under the guidance of King Philip, Clement summoned Fulk de Villaret, the Grand Master of the Hospitallers, and Jacques de Molay of the Templars, to meet him in Poitiers in France to discuss the force needed for a new crusade, and the unification of the Templars and the Hospitallers.

Jacques de Molay arrived in late 1306 or early 1307. He brought with him two memoranda. There is no record of what Fulk de Villaret brought, if anything. De Molay's first memorandum dealt with troop strength; he recommended a complement of 15,000 knights and 5,000 foot soldiers. The second memorandum argued strongly that the two Orders should not be united.

Historians are unanimous in their opinion that de Molay's arguments were very weak. Considering his age, and his longevity as a Grand Master, it is clear that he could not look upon the situation objectively.[4] As a result, his refusal, or inability, to realistically consider union with the Hospitallers is thought to have accelerated the Templars' downfall.

The proverb 'If someone says it's not the money, it's the principal, you know it's the money', would apply to King Philip. Philip was one of the last Capetian kings, a descendent of Hugh Capet whose reign and dynasty began in 987.[5] When Philip IV assumed the throne in 1285, he also assumed a substantial amount of debt that had been accumulated by his father, Philip III. The situation was made worse by Philip IV's efforts to expand his kingdom, and in particular the extraordinary expenses arising from a continuing series of battles and ongoing disputes with Flanders (now Belgium) to the north and Gascony in the south-west.[6]

Philip IV's considerable debts, and constant need for fresh capital, existed because in the thirteenth century there was no regular county-wide basis of taxation like there is today. The king's income was linked to revenue from his properties, rents arising from the enforcement of his feudal rights, and numerous iniquitous taxes. But this income was fairly constant and there was little else that could be used to reduce the debt. One of the main problems was the expense of his army. A king could often cover his living and household expenses with his income, but a minimal army at least had to be maintained, and this was a substantial draw on a king's finances. That is why taxation was often linked to a particular war or campaign. And, as Philip IV's kingdom expanded, so did his need for an army. As a result, he sought new taxes and novel methods to raise income.

One method of raising revenue was to levy a tax or a fee on an entire area. The reasons were usually trumped-up. For example, King Philip would declare an area heretical, and then confiscate the possessions of its residents. Rich groups, with little or no ability to retaliate, such as the Lombard merchants and bankers, would be singled out and then be economically ravaged by the king. One group ripe for taxation was the Jewish community; another was the clergy.

In 1307, Philip IV was so far in debt that he used a gimmick that almost resulted in his downfall. He debased the currency by a factor of about two-thirds. The result was catastrophic. Riots ensued throughout Paris that had to be put down by armed force. A number of alleged riot leaders were hanged as examples in order to prevent such riots from happening again. The devaluation was finally rescinded and France returned to a stable currency. But this left Philip with the problem of having little hard currency, i.e. gold and silver. In terms of the Templars, Philip's solution may have been right under his nose. During the riots, Philip sought refuge in the Paris Temple where he was apparently surrounded by untold wealth. Whether this was a motivating factor in the arrest of the Templars is unknown. But, the timing seems more than coincidental. And Philip was desperate to get out of debt. Further, Philip's financial problems, the unsuccessful currency devaluation and heavy taxation, may have been the result of decisions made and carried out by his advisors because Philip was more interested in hunting than in micromanaging financial details.[7]

By the latter part of 1307 Philip, or his advisors, had experimented with almost every financial expedient known to medieval rulers. Yet he had failed to achieve any significant, and lasting financial security.[8] Ultimately, Philip IV's last resort was the Knights Templar. As described by Malcolm Barber, 'The Templars, among others, were sacrificed as the monarchy thrashed around for an answer' to the king's significant financial problems.[9]

There is another very good argument as to why Philip chose to arrest the Templars. He wanted to control both the Templars and their wealth. Philip had initially tried to join the Templars with the intent of ultimately becoming the Grand Master. But he was denied membership.[10] After this, he was instrumental in the efforts to unite the Templars and the Hospitallers. His plan was to then make himself, or one of his sons, the 'Master-King' or 'Bellator Rex', the Warrior King of a united order.[11] But he was wholly unsuccessful, and with Clement V campaigning for a new crusade, King Philip would have had little reason, or excuse, to raise a substantial amount of money for a new military effort, or to have control of a major fighting force.

THE ARRESTS

The arrests were well planned and Philip did not act without first claiming to have a good reason: that 'persons worthy in the faith' had made a number of accusations that resulted in charges against the Templars.[12] According to Malcolm Barber, the charges were not made by Philip IV but by a number of others. They included the denial of Christ, spitting three times on the image of Christ, and a number of the acts that seemed to give the charges credibility. There was also the claim that Hugh de Châlons had been involved in a plot to kill King Philip.[13] Although the arrests and intended confiscation were consistent with Philip's previous practice of arresting heretics and seizing their property, he was well aware that they would not initially be a popular move. To counter this, he gave the impression that he doubted the truth of the charges. But he eventually came to the conclusion that he believed them. He then claimed to have met with the Pope, to have taken council from the prelates and barons as to how best to proceed, and ultimately acceded to the request of Guillaume de Paris, papal inquisitor in France.

But in fact, Pope Clement had not been asked about or even advised of the arrests. There apparently had been some discussion between the two men, but no mutual decision.[14]

On 14 September 1307, at the Abbey of Maubuisson near Pontoise, a few miles north of Paris, using the claim that 'persons worthy in faith' had made a number of accusations,[15] Philip IV ordered the preparation for the arrest of the Templars throughout his kingdom.

The order was made under seal, with the additional command that it was not to be opened until the night of Thursday 12 October.[16] The arrests began on Friday.

THE NUMBER OF ARRESTED TEMPLARS

An analysis of this subject is essential because there is a huge variance in the estimated number of arrested Templars in France. Also, it is necessary to know how many Templars could have escaped, and from this extrapolate how many of those could have gone to Scotland.

There are no existing records that state the number of Templars in France on 13 October 1307. The Templar records were secret and were not published. There was no census of Templars. All we have are estimates based on records of King Philip's trials and Clement V's inquisition. But one fact is certain. Among the knights arrested in France were the Grand Master Jacques de Molay, Hugh de Pairaud, visitor of France, and Geoffroi de Charney, Preceptor of Normandy. Gerard de Villiers, Preceptor of France, escaped. The questions are how many others were arrested, and how many escaped? The answers vary widely. Almost all of the readily accessible statistics deal with France.

One view is that on 13 October Jacques de Molay and virtually all of the 5,000 Templars in France were arrested by King Philip's men.[17] Only about twenty of these managed to escape.[18] Another view estimates the number of Templars arrested in France at 15,000, including knights, sergeants, chaplains, servants and laborers.[19] There is also the general view that the number of Templars in France was estimated to be around 2,000 by Clement V. All of them were said to have been arrested. But a fairly credible source puts the number between 500 and 700, of which only 50 to 100 were knights.[20]

According to Baigent and Leigh there were 556 full Templar preceptories in France and numerous other smaller holdings. They estimate that there were at least 3,200 Templars working in various capacities at these sites; of whom approximately 355 were knights and 936 were sergeants. It is generally believed that about 650 Templars were arrested. Baigent and Leigh estimate that, using these percentages, only 250 knights and sergeants were arrested, leaving 1,030 military members free.[21] Many of these men escaped from France and apparently went to Scotland and Portugal.

Historians appear to be relatively consistent in the estimate that 138 Templars were arrested in Paris. Of those, the range in age was from sixteen to eighty. They included priests, stewards, shepherds, laborers and carpenters. Only fifteen were knights.[22]

From the best estimates, it appears that from 210 to 355 knights avoided capture, as well as 556 to 936 sergeants, or totals that range from 766 to 1,291 knights and sergeants; an average of 1,030 fighting men. There were also approximately 1,550 other Templars who escaped. Of the 2,580 Templars in total, there is no way of knowing how many simply removed their tunics and melted into the local population, how many sailed to Portugal, and how many sailed for Scotland, Ireland and Wales. But if ten ships sailed for Scotland, this means that at least several hundred Templars arrived there, and they were all that was needed to help Robert the Bruce.

NOTES

1   There are many others who were involved in the Templars' arrests, but those listed are the ones who are essential to the Templars' flight to Scotland.

2   Barber, Malcolm, *The Trial of the Templars*, Cambridge University Press, Canto edition (Cambridge, 1993), p. 41.

3   Edwards, John, 'The Knights Templar in Scotland', *Transactions of the Scottish Ecclesiological Society*, Vol. IV (Aberdeen, 1912–1915), p. 40, citing Pollard, *Travels of Sir John Mandeville*, pp. 98–99.

4   Jacques de Molay was middle-aged when he became Grand Master.

5 Barber, *The Trial of the Templars*, p. 27. See Fawtier, R., *The Capetian Kings of France*, tr. L. Butler and R.J. Adam (London, 1960), pp. 55–56.

6 Barber, *The Trial of the Templars*, p. 32.

7 See Barber, *The Trial of the Templars*, pp. 28–30.

8 It is unknown whether it was Philip IV who developed direction and policy, or his ministers. It is known that he was served by two very competent and powerful advisors who held the position of 'Keeper of the Seal'. The first was Pierre Flote, who held the position from the 1290s until his death in 1302. He was followed by Guillaume de Nogaret, whose influence began in the late 1290s. He was ennobled by Philip in 1299 and became Keeper of the Seals in 1307, holding it until his death in 1313.

9 Barber, *The Trial of the Templars*, p. 32.

10 Howarth, *The Knights Templar*, p. 258.

11 Edith Simon, *The Piebald Standard, a Biography of the Knights Templar*, Little, Brown and Co. (Boston, 1959), describes King Philip's goals as being even more ambitious. At p. 227 Ms Simon states that 'he calmly proposed that:
– The Kings of France (beginning with himself) should be hereditary grand masters of the combined military orders;
– The incomes of all prelates, including archbishops, should be limited to a fixed minimum, the surplus to Rex Bellator for the conquest of the Holy Land;
– Propertied monks should be sent out into the world only for preaching and hearing confession, mendicant friars live immured, and their revenues beyond the same fixed annual rent likewise accrete to Rex Bellator's Coffers:
– The hereditary royal grand master should command four cardinal-votes at papal elections.'

12 Barber, *The Trial of the Templars*, p. 45.

13 Ibid., p. 46.

14 Ibid., pp. 47–48.

15 Ibid., p. 45.

16 Howarth, *The Knights Templar*, p. 247.

17 Ibid., p. 274.

18 Ibid., p. 278.

19 Read, Piers Paul, *The Templars*, St Martin's Press (New York, 1999), p. 264.

20 Partner, Peter, *The Knights Templar and their Myth*, rev. edn, Destiny Books (Rochester, Vermont, 1990), p. 59; and Forey, Alan, 'Towards a Profile of the Templars in the Early Fourteenth Century', in Malcolm Barber, ed.

The Military Orders, Fighting for the Faith and Caring for the Sick, Variorum (Aldershot, 1994), p. 198. Mr Forey's statistics are the result of an examination of the Templar trial deposition transcripts of between 506 and 681 Templars. The range exists because he included a study of the Templars examined in Paris in both 1307 and 1310–11. His range includes Templar examinations in Paris, Poiton, Clermont, Provence, the British Isles, Mas Den, Lerida, Cyprus, and Ales.

21 Baigent and Leigh, *The Temple and the Lodge*, pp. 65–66, citing 'extant charters'.

22 For example, see Burman, *The Templars, Knights of God*, p. 162, and Barber, Malcolm, *The Trial of the Templars*, Cambridge University Press, Canto edition (Cambridge, 1993), pp. 58–59.

6

THE TEMPLARS' FLIGHT TO SCOTLAND

Legend has it that even before King Philip IV signed the 14 September order, and before the arrests, some of the Templars, and a portion of the treasury that was kept in the Temple in Paris, were removed. Then, Hugh de Pairaud leaked the king's plans to the Templars. With this, the contents of the Paris Temple are said to have been taken, either overland by cart, or down the Seine by ship, to La Rochelle where the Templars harbored their fleet. From there, the knights and their riches sailed to Argyll, or to north-eastern Scotland, or to Portugal where both of the kings, Robert I in Scotland and Dinis in Portugal, were excommunicated, and neither supported the Pope or the French king. In addition, the Templars possessed preceptories, houses and tenements in both countries.

As to Portugal, it is well documented that after the Templars were dissolved, a new order, the Knights of Christ, was created there by King Dinis in 1319 with Templar property and personnel.[1] But the story of the Templars and Scotland is not well documented, and is considered by many to be nothing more than legend or myth. But, legends and myths often have some basis in history. And, there is much to support both the presence of the Templars in Scotland after 13 October 1307, and their participation in the Battle of Bannockburn.

Three basic facts are very surprising: Philip IV did not try to seize the Templars' substantial fleet; the Templars' fleet was never found[2]; and there appears to be no known discussion of the capture of the Templars' treasure after their arrest. But, there is evidence that the Templar treasure was taken out of France before 13 October.

THE TREASURY

What was in the Templars' treasury in the Paris Temple at the beginning of the fourteenth century? There is no clear answer to this question. There is no description of what was in the Paris Temple when Philip sought refuge there during the riots, or on 14 September 1307 when he signed the order for the warrants and the Templars' arrest. One view is that there was very little treasure, gold or silver, and that the wealth was concentrated in land.[3] On the other hand, the treasure owned by the Templars may have been substantial. For almost 200 years the Templars had received money as gifts and grants from the nobility, profits from their estates, booty from their battles, fees from their banking, and profits from their shipping. On top of this, their profits were not taxed.

Prior to the fall of Acre, the Templars primarily raised money for their expenses in the Middle East. Thus, the Paris Temple was the major bank and clearing house for the money going to Outremer. But, after 1291, those costs drastically decreased. In fact, the Templars even managed to take some of their treasury with them when they evacuated Acre.[4] But ultimately, the Middle East expenses amounted to little more than the cost of maintaining their headquarters on Cyprus. This meant that the Templars' primary purpose was the accumulation and maintenance of funds for the next crusade. As a result, the money held by the Templars in Paris must have been immense. It is not difficult to visualize it being enough to fill the numerous carts, or boats, that are said to have left Paris before 13 October.

How much of the treasure belonged to the Templars, and how much belonged to others is another unknown. Prior to 1292, the royal treasury was kept by the Templars at the Paris Temple, and was separately accounted for. This is evident from the fact that between 1292 and 1295, the bulk of Philip IV's treasury was moved from the Paris Temple to the Louvre. Then, after Philip's wars against the Flemish, and the French army's defeat at Courtrai, the Templars again became active in Philip's financial affairs, were responsible for much of Philip's treasury, and moved it back to the Paris Temple.

But the question of what was in the Temple on 13 October is not answered. There are numerous descriptions of the arrests. But there are none that describe Philip taking possession of the contents of the Paris Temple, or at least sealing the Temple and taking inventory of its contents. From this it would appear that there was no treasure for Philip to take, nor any gold or silver. Apparently, no Templar treasure existed in the Paris Temple on 13 September 1307. Of course, there may have been none to begin with. Jean Markale argues: '[T]he wealth of the Temple was primarily the enormous web it had spun over Europe and all the potential it held … [T]he Templars owned nothing but potential.'[5] But this overlooks the fact that there is no question the Templars did have possession of much of Philip's wealth, which could have been moved back to the Louvre. But this would have been recorded in Philip's accounts and been part of the evidence at the Templar trials.[6] Again, while there are numerous records of Templars being captured after 13 October, there is no record of the capture of any of the Templar treasure, religious artifacts or writings.

Whatever had been in the Paris Temple was not there the morning of 13 October. There is no reference in any available source that describes anything in the Paris Temple that morning. The only treasure ever mentioned is that at the headquarters on Cyprus.

FLIGHT

In his deposition, Hugh de Châlons stated that Gerard de Villiers had received word of the arrests and, with fifty Templars, had taken eighteen galleys and gone to sea.[7] This is a knight speaking of other knights. He does not describe who else, or how many were aboard. From this information there is a strong implication that many Templars did escape being arrested. Also, human nature being what it is, it would be safe to assume that when Philip IV gave the original order on 14 September, the news was quickly and quietly leaked to the Templars. But it was not simply a leak; Hugh de Pairaud apparently knew of the entire scheme, both from the point of view of King Philip IV and Pope Clement V. De Pairaud was part of the scheme because Pope Clement V believed that only Jacques de Molay would be arrested, and that de Pairaud would replace de Molay as Grand Master. But then de Pairaud learned of King Philip's order. The result is described by the Vatican historian Barbara Frale:

> When the true intention and scope of the king's scheme became evident, the inquisitor protested vehemently to the king – to no avail. The visitor general [Hugh de Pairaud] then understood the gravity of his mistake, realising that he had been used to strike a fatal blow against the Temple. Repenting his error, he tried to warn his brothers and exhort them to escape, but as he had isolated himself by his rivalry with Jacques de Molay, his appeal fell on deaf ears.[8]

This account is consistent with Hugh de Pairaud's encouragement to a young knight who wanted to leave the Order, to get out quickly because a 'catastrophe was at hand'.[9] Another Templar, who was later captured when he was begging in the streets of Paris, had escaped fifteen days before 13 October.[10] The time between King Philip's order and the arrests gave the Templars almost a month to get word to specific knights to start making preparations. These knights could then, in a very organized but subtle manner, move their wealth and treasure to the ports, and from there flee to the safe destinations of Portugal and Scotland.

There are several versions of how the Templar treasure could have left France in general, and Paris in particular. The best place to start is with a smaller portion of the treasure and an effort that was unsuccessful. The story appears to be credible because it is unembellished. According to Gerard de Sede in *Les Tempiers Sont Parmi Nous* (The Templars Are Among Us), Jean de Chalon stated that just before 13 October 1307 he took three carts containing the treasure of the Templars and left Paris the night before the arrests.[11] The contents of the carts were intended to go to La Rochelle for shipment abroad. Apparently the carts passed through the town of Gisors but never got any farther. The theory is that the treasure remains in Gisors in the underground passages that exist beneath the town, somewhere between the castle's keep and the town's church.[12]

The information about the flight of the Templars to Scotland is not simply myth and oral history. There was testimony after the arrests about Templar flight. But it did not occur until long after the interrogations had begun, and after some of the prisoners had been separated. After King Philip began his interrogation, torture and trials in Paris,

1. St Bernard, Abbot of Clairvaux (1090–1153). Fifteenth-century illumination by Jean Fauquet from the Hours of Etienne Chevalier. (Musée Conde, Chantilly, France/ Giraudon/Bridgeman Art Library)

2. The Burning of the Templars, c. 1308. Fourteenth-century engraving by French School. (British Library, London, UK, Bridgeman Art Library)

3. Jacques de Molay, c. 1243–1314. (Bridgeman Art Library, Getty Images)

4. The Old Temple Church at Temple. (Crown Copyright: Royal Commission on the Ancient and Historical Monuments of Scotland)

5. Castle Sween. (© 2008, Robert Ferguson)

6. Grave slab at Kilmartin
in display house. (© 2008,
Robert Ferguson)

7. Kilmartin Church. (© 2008, Robert Ferguson)

8. Grave slab at Kilmartin in the cemetery. (© 2008, Robert Ferguson)

9. Kilmory Church. (© 2008, Robert Ferguson)

10. Statue of Robert the Bruce.
(Photographed by John Boak,
National Trust for Scotland)

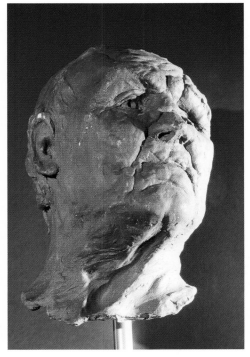

11. Bruce's forensic reconstructed head.
(Photographed by Allan Forbes, National
Trust for Scotland)

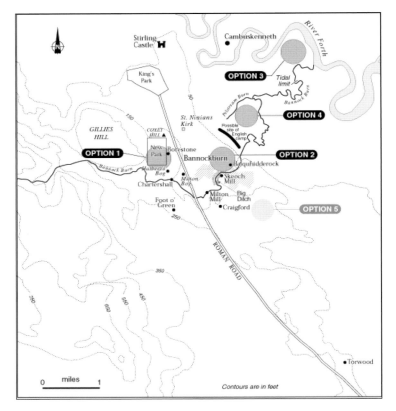

12. Map of options for locations for day two of the Battle of Bannockburn. (*The Battle of Bannockburn*, a Report for Stirling Council, by Fiona Watson, Ph.D. and Maggie Anderson, Ph.D.)

13. Rosslyn Chapel. (© Antonia Reeve/Rosslyn Chapel Trust)

14. General
inside view.
Looking east
towards the
main altar.
(© Antonia
Reeve/Rosslyn
Chapel Trust)

15. Sinclair burial stone. (© Antonia Reeve/Rosslyn Chapel Trust)

16. Knight on Horseback. (© Antonia Reeve/ Rosslyn Chapel Trust)

17. Green Man. (© Antonia Reeve/Rosslyn Chapel Trust)

Pope Clement V commenced a separate papal inquisition in Poitiers. This brought the trials in Paris to a halt. To placate Pope Clement, Philip brought seventy-two Templars to Poitiers so the trials could continue,[13] quelling the dispute between the king and the Pope as to whether the Templars should be tried in civil or ecclesiastical courts. The testimony confirming the flight of the Templars is found in the later trial depositions of several Templars. One of them was Hugh de Châlons. Several other knights corroborated his statements in their own inquisition depositions, that Gerard de Villiers had escaped with all the Templar treasure held by Hugh de Pairaud. These later admissions were made between 29 June and 2 July 1308 before Pope Clement V in Poitiers.

The Templar knights had waited until June of 1308 to describe the escapes and how the treasure had left the Paris Temple.[14] Apparently, these depositions were not given in the beginning because the Templars feared they would be killed by other imprisoned Templars if they revealed what had happened before the arrests.[15]

Again, there is evidence of substantial planning. Such plans would have been made by, or on behalf of, Jacques de Molay. As Grand Master, only he possessed the authority to arrange for the Templar treasure to be moved from Paris to La Rochelle and then shipped abroad. The evidence indicates that a majority of the ships sailed to Scotland.[16]

THE TEMPLARS SAIL TO SCOTLAND

While there is little direct evidence that the Templars sailed from La Rochelle to Scotland, it is known that a number of Templars in Italy fled to Scotland with Peter de Boulogne, the Grand Prelate and Procurator General at the Court of Rome.[17] If word got to Italy, it certainly circulated throughout France. Furthermore, the reality of the Templars fleeing from France is evident from the circumstances. With what is now known, there is little question that many of the Templars left France prior to 7 October 1307. They would not sail to England because England, and the Templars there, were closely aligned with Pope Clement V and with King Edward II. And, while King Edward initially refused to arrest the Templars, he did begin the process two months after 13 October 1307.

The evidence of the Templar wealth going to Scotland begins with the French inquisition depositions, which establish that the treasure was taken to the Templar ships from Paris in carts. There is also the prominent legend that between 14 September and 13 October the Templars loaded much of their wealth on barges, and left Paris on the Seine for their port at La Rochelle. Regardless of how the Templars and their treasure got to La Rochelle from Paris, a number of ships sailed south from there to Portugal. Another group, with the remainder of the treasure, sailed for Scotland.

But there are at least two other views as to how, and from where, the Templars left Europe for Scotland. One version has it that the Templars sailed from Aragon.[18] This view is propounded by Karen Ralls and is based on a statement by Heinrich Finke that 'fortified castles, changed goods into gold which could be more easily concealed and, it was suspected, charted a ship in which to make their escape'.[19] But the Templars were not significantly prosecuted in Spain. And this refers only to one ship which was chartered, rather than use of the Templar fleet.

Karen Ralls is also in agreement with the authors Alan Butler and Stephen Dafoe, who opine that the escape of a fleet on or near 13 October is illogical as the port would have been guarded and watched by Philip IV's soldiers.[20] But would it have been? The arrest order was under seal. Numerous ships guarding the port would have been very visible and would have alerted the ships' captains that something was planned. There is no record that Philip IV took any steps to alert anyone of the coming arrests. In fact, Jacques de Molay was honored as a pallbearer at the funeral of Philip IV's sister in law, Catherine of Valois, on 12 October 1307. So even when both Jacques de Molay and Philip IV knew of the coming arrests, neither of them did anything to alert the other, or anyone else.

There is also the theory concerning the fate of the Templar fleet, as put forth by Alan Butler and Stephen Dafoe.[21] They note that after the fall of Acre in 1297, the Templars' chief enterprises were commerce and banking. The Templar ships would not be sitting idly in La Rochelle or any other port. They would be under sail. If this were the case, then only a few of the ships would have been available. But the La Rochelle port, which had been given to the Templars by Eleanor of Aquitaine in the twelfth century, was part of a major harbor. The ships could have been held there as they came in without arousing any curiosity.

When the Templars left for Scotland, where did they go, and by what route? Michael Baigent and Richard Leigh argue that the route around the south of Ireland was the only one available:

> Edward's fleet, based on the east coast of England, effectively blocked the established trade routes between Flanders and Scottish ports such as Aberdeen and Inverness. Templar ships, moving northwards from La Rochelle or from the mouth of the Seine, could not have risked negotiating the Channel and the North Sea. Neither could they have proceeded through the Irish Sea, which was also effectively blocked by English naval vessel based at Ayer and at Carrickfergus in Belfast Lough. [22]

They then argue – quite forcefully – that the Templars sailed around western Ireland, to northern Ireland, and then north up the sound of Jura to Argyll. [23] This is based on the presence of Templar gravestones in the churchyards at Kilmartin and Kilmory, and the presence of a Templar-like cross in the church at Kilmory. [24] Baigent and Leigh further argue that the Templars probably landed at Castle Sween (Figure 5), which is located between Kilmartin and Kilmory, and is said to be the oldest castle on the Scottish mainland. [25] There is also said to be evidence of Templar gravestones in Kilmartin. One example is the pristine grave slab in the exhibition building behind Kilmartin Church (Figure 6). The exhibition building is to the left of the church at Kilmartin in Figure 7. The slab is in the Templar tradition and is believed to be from the fourteenth century. Many comparable grave slabs, such as the one shown in Figure 8, are found in the Kilmartin cemetery. Other evidence of Templar presence in Argyll is said to be found in the churchyard and cemetery of the thirteenth-century church at Kilmory, which is shown in Figure 9.

But all of this overlooks the fact that the Templars had a substantial estate in Ayre, and that until 13 October the arrest order was sealed. If they had left La Rochelle even one or two days earlier, they would have been well on their way and well ahead of King Philip's arrest warrants. With this scenario, the Templars could have simply sailed through the Irish Sea, into the North Channel, past the Firth of Clyde and Ayre, and then north up the sound of Jura to Argyll. The arrest of the Templars was not yet common knowledge. And when the arrest order arrived in

England, Edward II would not recognize or enforce it. It was not until 26 December 1307, in response to the papal bull *Pastoralis praeeminentiae*, that he reversed himself and ordered the Templars be arrested.[26] In this context, the Templar fleet would have sailed right past the English.

It is also very possible that a portion of the fleet sailed up the east coast of Scotland. In line with this, a French Masonic tradition states that the records and wealth of the Templars were carried on nine ships from La Rochelle to the Isle of Mey in the Firth of Forth. This tradition is supported by eight Templar tombstones that have been found in Currie near Edinburgh, and in Westkirk near Culross in Fife.[27]

There is also the view that the Templar fleet sailed from France to the Orkney Islands under an agreement with William St Clair.[28] This view is undoubtedly based on the longstanding belief that the Templar founder, Hughes de Payens, had been married to a member of the Saint Clair family, Catherine de Saint-Clair. The theory goes on that this marriage resulted in a lasting bond between the Saint-Clairs (Sinclairs) and the Templars. But again, recent research indicates that this theory may not be valid, and that the wife of Hughes de Payens was Elisabeth de Chappes.[29]

But there are several other credible arguments that support the Templars landing in north-eastern Scotland. David Hatcher Childress, in his introduction to Addison's *The History of the Knights Templar*, and Baigent and Leigh in *The Temple and the Lodge*, argue that the Templars left Europe en masse, including their ships in northern Europe and in the Mediterranean. From this, the ships from northern Europe could easily have landed well north of the Firth of Forth or in the Orkney Islands.

But, there is little physical evidence that the Templars landed or lived in north-east Scotland as early as the start of the thirteenth century. The evidence supports their landing in Argyll, and Fife near the head of the Firth of Forth. In addition, the ships in the Mediterranean would have sailed through the straits of Gibraltar, up the west coast of Ireland to Donegal and Ulster, where Templar properties were located. It was from the northern Ireland preceptories that arms smuggling to Argyll was common.

Finally, in terms of flight from the continent, there is the one fact that, if true, is the lynch pin: that Peter de Boulogne fled from Rome to Scotland with several others and took refuge with their northern brethren.[30]

In England it is believed that many of the Templars 'successfully evaded capture by obliterating all marks of their previous profession; some had escaped in disguise to the wild and mountainous parts of Wales, Scotland, and Ireland.'[31] Assuming there were 144 Templars in England, only twenty of them were knights.[32] But if only six knights were arrested, then a significant number of them fled, and in all probability they fled to Scotland. Wales had a very small Templar presence, and Ireland was aligned with Pope Clement V. And even without their mantles, most Templar Knights would be very conspicuous, having lived and socialized only with other knights.

Despite all the arguments supporting the theory that the Templars sailed to Scotland, there are many who believe the Templars did not escape from France, did not sail to Scotland, and did not fight with Robert the Bruce at Bannockburn.[33]

Some posit that Argyll, where the Templars are reputed to have landed, was not clearly demarcated, and that because of the conflict between the MacDonalds and the MacDougalls it was not the isolated safe harbor it is reported to have been.

Argyll now extends from the Kintyre Peninsula in the south to well north of the town of Oban and Loch Awe. In 1301 Edward I of England had established an alliance with both the MacDonalds of Islay in the south, and the MacDougalls of Lorn, an area to the north which surrounds the city of Oban at the head of the Firth of Lorne. But by 1306, the leader of the MacDonalds was Angus Og, who was a supporter of Robert the Bruce.[34] Thus, in 1306 Bruce's supporters controlled both the opening of the sound of Jura and the Isle of Islay on the west side of the sound. The areas held by the MacDougalls were mainly around Loch Awe and Lock Etive to the east and north of Oban. If the Templars were intent on joining Robert the Bruce, they could easily have sailed up the sound of Jura. The logical landing place would be the twelfth-century Castle Sween, between Kilmartin and Kilmory.

Others erroneously believe that the excommunication of Robert the Bruce was an individual matter and applied only to Bruce and not to his country. This would be true if Bruce were not the King of Scotland. But he was. In addition, the Pope had placed an interdict on Scotland.[35] As a result, the excommunication applied to Bruce, his country and his subjects. While Scotland could not join the comity of nations, the Church of Scotland continued, and the people continued to attend, because the Scots recognized the Church as the Scottish Church which placed the independence of Scotland above the remote, Italian Pope.[36] After Bruce had killed John 'The Red' Comyn, Bishop Wishart in Glasgow accepted Bruce's Confession and gave him absolution. Bruce, in return swore to defend the Scottish Church.[37] Accordingly, the Pope and his orders were simply disregarded. Everyday life, including worship in the local church, continued. It was several decades later that the Pope ultimately lifted the excommunication, and the Scots and the Scottish Church again recognized the Pope's authority.

It is true that the last major military engagement in which the Knights Templar were involved took place in 1291 at Acre, and that the losses of the Knights Templar were very heavy. It has been argued that this led to the virtual dissipation of the front-line Templar fighting forces and that the Templars were therefore in no position to aid the Scots at Bannockburn.[38]

The only reference to a possible Templar fighting force was their inclusion in a group known as 'the small folk',[39] who came charging over the hill at the end of the Battle of Bannockburn.[40] This can hardly be termed a 'front-line fighting force'. A front-line fighting force was not what the Templars brought to Scotland. As demonstrated in the Appendix, the vast majority of the knights who fled to Scotland would have been veterans. The majority came with many years of service.[41] They had been part of one of the most effective fighting units in the world, and with them came two essential elements for an effective army: knowledge and wealth. While Bruce needed warriors, he specifically needed well-trained warriors, and the veteran Templars could provide the training. Further, before Bannockburn Bruce's troops had primitive homemade weapons. They needed uniform, professionally made equipment and the funds that could provide them. Scotland was a poor, war-ravaged country. There was barely enough food for the people who lived there. But with their numerous estates and land in Scotland, and money to import food, the Templars could provide the enormous amount of rations necessary to feed up to 6,000 men for several months.

Perhaps the strongest argument made against a Templar presence in Scotland is the simple lack of contemporary written evidence of it.[42] But the lack of such written evidence is not surprising. The Templars had escaped from France, Spain and Italy. There were numerous Scottish clans and groups that supported England. The last thing the Templars would want to be is too visible. This is where the fact that they were not only warriors but monks becomes relevant. The Templars lived austere and spartan lives. They sought to achieve results, not laudatory recognition. In addition, very few could write, and therefore little was written. The only individuals who were written about were leaders such as Bruce, his brothers, Sir William St Clair, Angus Og, and the persons who were present during significant events such as Bishop Wishart, or Roger Kirkpatrick, who is believed to have ultimately stabbed John Comyn. This practice is demonstrated by the description of what happened during the battle at the pass at Brander. The MacDougalls had 2,000 concealed men guarding the pass who were discovered by one of Bruce's 'scouts'. With this knowledge, Bruce sent 'James Douglas' with a party of light-armed archers around, up, and behind the MacDougalls. History did not record the name of the scout. But there is no doubt as to who led the forces that surprised and defeated the MacDougalls. Similarly, no one will ever know the names of the warrior-monks who assisted Robert the Bruce.

Finally, there were no books written about Robert the Bruce or Bannockburn between 1305 and 1315. The closest relevant documents are chronicles that were written decades later. There is little chance that knights who were under the threat of death, or worse – being skinned or disemboweled, both of which were common in Europe in that era – would do anything to draw attention to themselves.

The Templars would have joined Bruce to fight and lend their skills and their resources. Between his coronation in 1305 and the Templar arrests in 1307, Bruce led what can be called a rag-tag bunch that spent most of its time hiding. In August 1306 John MacDougall of Lorn defeated Bruce at the battle of Dail Righ (now Daly, north of Ayre and near the Firth of Clyde). But then, in May 1308 at Inveruri, while Bruce was very sick, his troops under the leadership of his brother Edward outsmarted John Comyn, Earl of Buchan. Bruce's men were substantially outnumbered and had run out of provisions. But Edward used a novel approach. He advanced with a fabricated show of strength that allowed Bruce's men to march back into the mountains and safety.

After he had regained his strength, Bruce used this same bravado to defeat John Comyn. (After this battle, there is no further report of a lack, or shortage of provisions.) Then, in 1309 Bruce defeated the MacDougalls at the pass at Brander. In two and a half years Robert the Bruce had transformed from a hunted fugitive to the ruler of two-thirds of Scotland. And as Ronald McNair Scott recognized, this must be first credited to Robert the Bruce himself. 'But no man can operate in a vacuum.'[43] Bruce was surrounded by excellent leaders. He had the unwavering support of the Church of Scotland, and the support of his subjects who could foresee a free Scotland. But two and a half years is a very short time to go from fugitive to victor in a poor country, where food was scarce, where weapons were crudely made at home, where there were few roads, and where there was no efficient means of communication. From that point of view, one should consider that Bruce must have had something else; and that would be funds and training. These elements could only have been supplied by the Templars.

NOTES

1 Also known as the Order of Christ.
2 Baigent, Michael, and Leigh, Richard, *The Temple and the Lodge*, Arcade Publishing, Inc. (New York, 1989), p. 8.
3 Burman, Edward, *The Templars: Knights of God*, Destiny Books (Rochester, 1986), p. 173, articulates a view held by several authors that the Templars possessed little movable property – treasure, cash, gold and silver. But this fact is taken from inventories that were compiled after the Templars' downfall.
4 Nicholson, Helen, *The Knights Templar, A New History*, Sutton Publishing (Gloucestershire, 2001), p. 198.
5 Markale, Jean, *The Templar Treasure at Gisors*, Inner Traditions International (Rochester, 2003), p. 161.
6 Ibid., pp. 37–38.
7 Barber, Malcolm, *The Trial of the Templars*, p. 101, citing Finke, H., *Papsttum and Untergang des Templerordens*, vol. 2 (Munster, 1907), pp. 337–339.
8 Frale, Barbara, *The Knights Templar: The Secret History Revealed*, Arcade Publishing (New York, 2009), p. 157. Barbara Frale is a member of the staff of the Vatican Secret Archives, and is a specialist on the Templars, the crusades and the papacy.
9 Simon, Edith, *The Piebald Standard, a Biography of the Knights Templar*, Little, Brown and Co. (Boston, 1959), p. 267.

10 Barber, *The Trial of the Templars*, p. 46.

11 Jean de Chalon came back to France and was arrested. This testimony was part of his trial transcript.

12 Markale, *The Templar Treasure at Gisors*, pp. 48–49.

13 Barber, *The Trial of the Templars*, p. 98.

14 Ibid., p. 101; Finke, *Papsttum and Untergang*, pp. 337–339.

15 Ibid.

16 See Gardner, Laurence, *Bloodline of the Holy Grail*, pp. 271–272.

17 Coutts, Rev. Alfred, *The Knights Templar in Scotland* (Edinburgh, 1890), p. 18.

18 Ralls, Karen, *The Templars and the Grail*, Quest Books (Wheaton, 2003), pp. 26–27.

19 Ibid.

20 Butler, Alan and Dafoe, Stephen, *The Warriors and the Bankers*, Templar Books (Ontario, 1998).

21 Butler and Dafoe, *The Warriors and the Bankers*, pp. 23–30.

22 Baigent and Leigh, *The Temple and the Lodge*, p. 65.

23 Ibid., p. 71.

24 Ibid., pp. 5–11.

25 Ibid., p. 12.

26 Ibid., pp. 193, 195.

27 Sinclair, Andrew, *The Sword and the Grail*, Birlinn Limited (Edinburgh, 2002), p. 45.

28 Sora, Steven, *The Lost Treasure of the Knights Templar*, Destiny Books (Rochester, 1999), p. 109.

29 Coppens, Philip, *The Stone Puzzle of Rosslyn Chapel*, Frontier Publishing (the Netherlands, 2004), p. 14, citing the biography *Hughes de Payens, Chevalier Champenoise, Fondateur de L'Order des Templiers* (Troyes: editions de la Maison Boulager, 1997).

30 *Statutes of the Religious and Military Order of The Temple, as Established in Scotland with An Historical Notice of the Order*, 'Historical Notice of the Order' printed by authority of the Grand Conclave, 1843, 2nd edn, Alex, Laurie and Co. (Edinburgh, 1964), p. vii.

31 Addison, Charles G., *The History of the Knights Templar* (originally published in London, 1842), Adventure Unlimited Press (Kempton, 2001), p. 213.

32 This is the lowest number cited by any of the major authors, but it was obtained by Clarence Perkins after a thorough examination of the various sources. Clarence Perkins, 'The Knights Templar in the British Isles', *The English Historical Review*, Vol. 25, No. 98 (July 1910), p. 222. Lord,

Evelyn, *The Knights Templar in Britain*, p. 194, states that 153 Templars were arrested in England, and Charles G. Addison in *The History of the Knights Templar*, p. 213, states that 229 Templars were arrested in England.

33 See: Cooper, Robert L.D., *The Rosslyn Hoax? Viewing Rosslyn Chapel from a new perspective*, Lewis (UK, 2006).

34 Ibid., p. 215.

35 Gerber, Pat, *Stone of Destiny*, Conongate Books Ltd (Edinburgh, 1997), p. 113.

36 Magnusson, Magnus, *Scotland: The Story of a Nation*, Atlantic Monthly Press (New York, 2000), p. 187.

37 Scott, Ronald McNair, *Robert the Bruce, King of Scots*, Carroll & Graf Publishers (New York, 1996), p. 74.

38 Cooper, *The Rosslyn Hoax?* p. 222.

39 Magnusson, *Scotland*, pp. 185–186.

40 Cooper, *The Rosslyn Hoax?* p. 221.

41 Forey, Alan, 'Towards a Profile of the Templars in the Early Fourteenth Century', in Malcolm Barber, ed. *The Military Orders, Fighting for the Faith and Caring for the Sick*, Variorum (Aldershot, 1994), p. 198.

42 Ibid., pp. 217–218.

43 Scott, *Robert the Bruce*, p. 116.

7

SCOTLAND'S TEMPLAR INQUISITION

The inquisition in Scotland involved a lot of activity, but in the end, unlike the inquisition in France, things ended well.

On 13 October 1307, when Phillip IV of France arrested the Templars of France as heretics and began severe torture to secure immediate confessions, he also sent a clerk to England to urge a similar policy from Edward II.[1] At first, King Edward II of England did not follow Philip's example because he did not give the report any credit. Specifically, on 30 October 1307 he told Philip IV that he could not give easy credence to the accusations. On 4 December Philip IV sent duplicate letters to the kings of Portugal, Castile, Aragon and Naples strenuously defending his order. It was not until 26 December, in response to the papal bull *Pastoralis praeeminentiae*, that Edward II reversed himself and ordered the Templars arrested in 'the quickest and best way'.[2] But Edward still did not enforce Philip's order. Then, on 8 January 1308, after strenuous urging from Philip and Pope Clement V,[3] and the personal petition by three bishops, the arrests were carried out.[4] Two hundred and twenty-nine Templars were taken into custody in England. But many more either fled to Scotland and Ireland, or simply removed their Templar tunics and attempted to disguise themselves. Those that went to Scotland undoubtedly went to the northern highlands because those in the lowlands were subject to Edward II's inquisition. The Templars' allegiance was to both the Temple in London and to the king. The Master or Preceptor of Scotland not only reported to the Master of the Temple in London, but he was required to pledge an oath of allegiance to Edward II. This applied to Brian de Jay who swore his oath in 1291, and to his successor John de Sauté who swore a similar oath to Edward I in 1296.

The arrests in Scotland did not begin until 17 November 1309, when the inquisitor for Scotland, Master John de Solerio, papal chaplain and canon of Hereford, began traveling north from London.[5] At the same time, John de Segrave, the English guardian of Scotland, was ordered to arrest the Templars in Scotland and hold them for examination. The proceedings began later in the month at Holyrood Abbey in Edinburgh by John de Solerio and William Lamberton, the Bishop of St Andrews. The inquisition was hurried. Edinburgh, like most of the Scottish lowlands, was subject to English rule. But Robert the Bruce was gaining strength in the north, and in Galloway and Carrick. And the area around Edinburgh was subject to continuous incursions by Bruce. Consequently, an attack by Bruce was expected at any time. Add to this the fact that Edward II's attention was also focused on possible negotiations for a truce with Scotland. In November, when the inquisition in Scotland began, Edward II was being approached by ambassadors from France who came to mediate between Edward and Robert the Bruce.

Only two Templar Knights were called before the inquisition in Scotland. They were Walter de Clifton and William de Middleton. Walter de Clifton was the last Master of the Templars in Scotland at Balantrodoch. In addition to three years at Balantrodoch, he had spent three years at Temple Newsam in Yorkshire, one in London, and three at Rockley in Wiltshire and at Aslackby in Lincolnshire. William de Middleton had lived both at Balantrodoch and Maryculter. Both were Englishmen by birth, both had been invested at English preceptories, and both reported to the Master in London. The reason that only two Templars were arrested is that, according to Walter de Clifton, the other Templars had fled beyond the sea. One was his predecessor, John de Huseflete, who had been the previous Master of Balantrodoch. He simply threw off his habit and 'fled from justice'.[6] The other was Thomas Totti, who was possibly the preceptor at Maryculter. Both were Englishmen. Yet according to James Burnes, the learned French writer Raymouard states that having deserted the Temple, 'they ranged themselves under the Banners of Robert the Bruce'.[7] From this it is not difficult to hypothesize that the Templar leadership in England, and their attendants, fled and joined the Templars in Scotland. Those in Scotland simply continued on in their roles as a sergeant or bailli, or traveled a few short miles to northern Scotland to use their skills there where they were needed.

The inquisition in Scotland was unlike those conducted by Philip IV or Edward II, but not significantly different from that conducted by the three cardinals at Chinon Castle in Tours, France. As part of the trials conducted by Philip IV, the Templars were subjected to, or threatened with, extreme and unrelenting torture. It was applied until the interrogator obtained the desired confession. While England banned the use of torture, pressure from the French king and the Pope resulted in its use. But no torture was used in Scotland. This is evident from what has been written about the inquisition in Scotland, and the fact that none of the witnesses made any of the incredible confessions that were obtained in France, or even England.

In addition to the two Templars, there were nearly fifty witnesses at Holyrood. These included both lay and clerical witnesses. What is significant is that none of the sergeants or baillis were arrested or testified. The absence of testimony by Templar sergeants, chaplains and staff is highlighted by the fact that there was a consistent theme among all of the testifiers that was wholly unfavorable to the Templars: that is, their dislike for, and their suspicion of the Templars. Several of the witnesses, including William de Preston and William de St Clair, accused the Templars of unjust greed and lack of hospitality. William de St Clair's brother, Henry de St Clair, also gave evidence against the Templars.[8] But Adam de Wedale was very specific. He testified that 'The order is defamed in manifold ways by unjust acquisitions, for it seeks to appropriate the goods and property of its neighbors justly and unjustly with equal indifference, and does not cultivate hospitality except towards the rich and powerful, for fear of dispersing its possessions in alms.'[9] But, with all this said, it must be noted that the Templar Knights in Scotland were English who spoke English, Norman French, or Latin, and not Gaelic.[10]

Of all the accusations, Clifton and Middleton admitted only that the Masters in London usurped the priestly power of absolution. But this may well have been in conjunction with the Master's disciplinary power of giving absolution from offenses against the Rule of the Order, and not absolution from crimes of violence that were only offered by priests. Otherwise, virtually all of the significant adverse testimony was either hearsay, or unsubstantiated.

The suspicions held by the public apparently arose from the secrecy of the Templars' initiation ceremony. Walter de Clifton admitted that this impression was true, but then gave a detailed and picturesque account of the ceremony:

> After telling some Templars of his wish to become one of them, and being at first discouraged and told that he sought a great and hard thing in desiring to give up his own will and enter into obedience, he was at length introduced to a chapter held by the English master at the Lincolnshire preceptory of Bruce. There, with joined hands and on bended knees, he asked to have the habit and brotherhood of the order. The master questioned him as to possible impediments – was he in debt? Was he affianced to a woman? Had he any secret infirmity of body? When these questions had been answered in the negative, and the brethren present had given their consent to his reception, the ceremony of initiation at once took place, for with the Templars there was no period of probation. Still on his knees, the postulant promised to be servant for ever to the Master and brethren in defense of the Holy land, and swore to God and the Virgin, placing his hand beneath a copy of the Gospels which had a cross depicted on it, that he would live in chastity, poverty, and obedience. Then the master handed him the mantle and cap of the order, gave him the kiss of peace, and making him sit down upon the ground, recited and explained to him certain of the rules of discipline.[11]

Of the fifty witnesses, none of their testimony established the guilt of the two Templar Knights. All it did was confirm that the Templars had lost their aura of honor and virtue, and were intensely disliked. Basically, the public was suspicious of what they saw. The Abbots of Dunfermline, Holyrood and Newbattle had no knowledge of any evidence against the two Templars regarding the charges in the articles. They could only speak of the secret and nocturnal activities and thought them 'most suspicious'.[12] Brother Adam de Wedale, a monk of Newbattle who was the eighth witness, stated that the Templars gave no alms and 'shewed no hospitality, save for the rich and powerful'.[13] He made no mention of heresy, but stressed that the knights, and in particular the preceptors, displayed pride and avarice, and sought aggrandizement of the Order and the enrichment of themselves. Nine or ten of the Templars' tenants testified about the secrecy of the Templar chapters. They also attested that the Templars gave and received lay absolution. But they had no first-hand knowledge. In answer to the outrageous charge that the Templars burned the bodies of their diseased brethren, and then made powder of the ashes for the initiates to drink to confirm a pledge of secrecy, the chaplain of Liston stated only that the Templars had always been hostile to the Church. As to the charge, he said he had not heard of any Templars dying a natural death, or seen a Templar grave.

The most serious or heinous crime was heresy. It was looked upon as being more serious than crimes of moral turpitude or depravity. 'Suspected heretics had practically no legal rights and their capture was the highest duty of all secular officials.'[14] King Philip IV of France's fourteenth charge was that the Templars worshipped a certain cat that appeared at times in their chapters. But, it has been noted that the testimony at Holyrood 'would not suffice to hang a cat', let alone a Templar Knight.[15] The only charge that could be made, and it was by the local clergy who observed it, was that confession and absolution was taken and given by the preceptors. But as monks, they received the confessions of brothers and dispensed punishment as appropriate. In fact, when the Templars received their Rule in 1128, the rites of confession, absolution and satisfaction were entrusted to the head of the local Temple House who was considered to be a monk with semi-sacerdotal character. Further, the rites were not administered to anyone outside the Order.

Even Brian de Jay's name was brought up during the inquisition. Apparently his reputation and the general dislike for him was so great that it continued for years after his death. One witness asserted that Brian de Jay had denied Christ to be the true God and man. The witness also stated that Brian de Jay had claimed the least hair on a Saracen's beard was worth a Templar's whole body. Another witness said that on a winter's day beggars asked for alms for the sake of our lady. De Jay is said to have thrown a farthing in freezing mud and made the beggars grovel and pick them up with their mouths.

Ultimately, the decision of John de Solerio and William Lamberton was like that of the three cardinals at Chinon Castle. None of the charges were established and the Templars were found innocent. After the inquisition, William de Middleton was sent to the Cistercian monastery of Roche where he spent three years on a small pension. Then, after a papal decree giving ex-Knights Templar the right to live in the religious house of their choice, he moved to the Augustinian house of Bridlington, and then to a monastery in Coldingham Priory where he died in 1325.[16] Walter de Clifton was sent to and remained at Shelford.[17]

There is always the question of the number of Templars in Scotland. If one views the question from the point of view that only two Templars were available to be questioned at the Scottish inquisition, it would appear that there were only a few Templars in Scotland. This may well have applied to the number of knights. But with the numerous Templar properties in Scotland, there had to be a number of sergeants and baillis. The question then becomes, what happened to them? One answer is in the transcript of Walter de Clifton, who stated that 'the rest of the Brethren had fled and dispersed themselves *propter scandalium exortum contra ordinem*.[18] This theory concludes that they then lent their skills and resources to Robert the Bruce.

The other is a belief firmly held by some of today's Knights Templar in Scotland. Their belief begins with the fact that the inquisitor, William Lamberton, the Bishop of St Andrews, was loyal to Robert the Bruce and the independence of Scotland. The 'Good' Sir James Douglas, probably Bruce's closest friend, and known to the English as 'The Black Douglas', had been Bishop Lamberton's protégé. Bishop Lamberton was present at Bruce's coronation. What is known is that the transcript of the testimony between the bishop and the two Templars was sent to King Edward II and the Pope. But there may have been an understanding (that was off the record) that if the Templars would supply Robert the Bruce with arms, money and expertise, the Scots 'will give you sanctuary in the only land where the Pope's writ does not run'.[19]

Is the story true? The belief that the Templars fought for Robert the Bruce is not new. In 1898 Robert Aitken wrote: 'Some [Templars] like John de [Huseflete], fled over the sea, probable to Norway or Denmark, while others, perhaps, found a refuge in the little army of the excommunicated King Robert, whose fear of offending the French monarch would doubtless be vanquished by his desire to secure a few capable men-at-arms as recruits.'[20] In 1890, the Rev. Alfred Coutts went even further when he stated: 'But it is generally believed that the Scottish Knights of the Temple joined the National Standard under Bruce, and fought with him, till he won the freedom of the Kingdom at Bannockburn.'[21] It is certain that the former grants in favor of the Temple were confirmed by Bruce and his successors. To some extent the agreement between Bishop Lamberton and the Templars could be true, in light of the fact that in France all levels of Templars, knights, sergeants, chaplains, and workers, were arrested. But in Scotland only two knights were arrested. In France they were tortured and, as shown in Figure 2, burned at the stake. In England there was some torture at the insistence of the Pope, and some Templars were jailed, but none of this happened in Scotland. All that happened to the two knights was what is described in modern terms as 'they were brought in for questioning'.

NOTES

1 Perkins, Clarence, 'The Trial of the Knights Templar in England', *The English Historical Review*, Vol. 24, No. 95 (July 1909), p. 432.

2 Baigent, Michael and Leigh, Richard, *The Temple and the Lodge*, Arcade Publishing (New York, 1989), pp. 193, 195.

3 Aitken, Robert, 'The Knights Templar in Scotland', *The Scottish Review* (July 1898), p. 28.

4 Addison, Charles G., *The History of the Knights Templar* (originally published in London, 1842), Adventures Unlimited Press (Illinois, 2001), p. 226.

5 Barber, Malcolm, *The Trial of the Templars*, Cambridge University Press, Canto edition (Cambridge, 1993), p. 203.

6 Edwards, John, 'The Knights Templar in Scotland', *Transaction of the Scottish Ecclesiological Society*, Vol. IV (Aberdeen, 1912–1915), p. 43.

7 Burnes, James, *Sketch of the History of the Knights Templar*, Wm. Blackwood & Sons (Edinburgh, 1840), p. 60.

8 Lord, Evelyn, *The Knights Templar in Britain*, Pearson Education Limited (Edinburgh, 2002), p. 153.

9 Edwards, John, 'The Templars in Scotland in the Thirteenth Century', *Scottish Historical Review* (1908), p. 21, citing *Processus factus contra Templarios in Scotia* from The Spottiswoode Miscellany, Vol. ii, p. 14.

10 Lord, *The Knights Templar in Britain*, p. 109.

11 Aitken, 'The Knights Templar in Scotland', pp. 30–31. This account is far different from those in France where torture was common. Before the arrests, the Pope had been informed by the Templars' visitor general, Hugh de Pairaud, that novices were commanded to commit acts of heresy by denying Christ and spitting on the cross. It is believed that this was done as part of a second initiation ceremony to impress on the initiate the need for absolute

obedience to superiors. Frale, Barbara, *The Knights Templar: The Secret History Revealed*, Arcade Publishing (New York, 2009), pp. 157, 163–164.

12 Ibid., p. 31.

13 Ibid., pp. 31–32.

14 Edwards, 'The Templars in Scotland in the Thirteenth Century', p. 21.

15 Edwards, 'The Knights Templar in Scotland', p. 44.

16 Ibid., p. 34.

17 Cooper, Robert L.D., *The Rosslyn Hoax? Viewing Rosslyn Chapel from a new perspective*, Lewis (UK, 2006), pp. 214–215.

18 *Statutes of the Religious and Military Order of The Temple, as Established in Scotland with An Historical Notice of the Order*, 'Historical Notice of the Order' printed by authority of the Grand Conclave, 1843, 2nd edn, Alex, Laurie and Co. (Edinburgh, 1964), p. vii, citing Wilkins' Concilia.

19 McKerracher, Archie, 'Bruce's Secret Weapon', *The Scots Magazine* (June 1991), pp. 261, 265; Gerber, Pat, *Stone of Destiny*, Conongate Books Ltd (Edinburgh, 1997), p. 130.

20 Aitken, 'The Knights Templar in Scotland', p. 34.

21 Coutts, Rev. Alfred, *The Knights Templar in Scotland* (Edinburgh, 1890), p. 11.

8

THE KNIGHTS TEMPLAR AND THE BATTLE OF BANNOCKBURN

Were the Knights Templar at Bannockburn? No one knows, or ever will. It is easy to say that they were not at Bannockburn because in 1314 nothing was written that says they were there. None of the later chronicles about Robert the Bruce describe the Templars as being present there, but for at least the last 2–300 years, writers have hinted that they were. And there has always been the myth. While there is no way to know if the Templars were at Bannockburn, there is circumstantial evidence, and one can make an argument that they were there. The purpose of this chapter is to make that argument. In a book about the Templars and Scotland, it is an argument that has to be made. The final decision as to whether the Templars were there or not is for the reader to make. Regardless of the reader's conclusion, the facts and events surrounding the battle must be looked at from a different perspective. The conclusion drawn from this perspective is new, and differs from previous versions.

The argument for the Templar presence at Bannockburn does not diminish Robert the Bruce's ability. He was one of the most formidable army commanders of the age. His statue at Bannockburn correctly depicts him for what he was, a highly effective leader, planner and motivator (see Figure 10). Bruce's deeds as a warrior are shown in the forensic reconstruction of his head, which reveals a broken cheekbone, a sword wound to his head, a distended eye socket and upper jaw damage (see Figure 11).[1]

After his coronation, Robert the Bruce was still little more than a fugitive. He had few men-at-arms, provisions were scarce, and much of the nobility in Scotland sided with his enemy, the Comyns. His first victory came in March 1307 at the Glen Trool, where he and a force of between 100 and 300 men, and a great deal of surprise and ferocity, forced the Earl of Pembroke and 1,500 men to flee. The battle was really a skirmish with few fatalities. But it is memorialized with a monument that gives the skirmish significance.

IN LOYAL REMEMBRANCE OF ROBERT THE BRUCE KING OF SCOTS WHOSE VICTORY IN THIS GLEN OVER AN ENGLISH FORCE IN MARCH 1307 OPENED THE CAMPAIGN OF INDEPENDENCE WHICH HE BROUGHT TO DECISIVE CLOSE AT BANNOCKBURN ON THE 24th JUNE, 1314.

Bruce's next victory came on 10 May 1307 at Loudon Hill. This time the Earl of Pembroke brought 3,000 men. But Bruce had chosen his ground well, and was able to force the first wave of Englishmen into a relatively narrow area. Here he had dug three ditches. When Pembroke's mounted squadron arrived at the first ditch, chaos reigned. This time with 600–700 men, Bruce was again able to rout the English.

Unfortunately for the English, and fortunately for Bruce, Edward I, known as 'the Hammer of the Scots', died on 11 July 1307. The English forces withdrew and Bruce was given some breathing room.

In the autumn of 1307, when the Templars were either being arrested in France or fleeing from Philip IV, Bruce's troops numbered around 700.[2] But after numerous skirmishes and battles they were worn out. Bruce was so weary that he became ill, many say close to death. He spent the winter at Inverurie and eventually recovered.

It would be convenient to think that the Templars left France and joined Bruce at Inverurie. But Bruce and his men were then on the run from John Comyn, the Earl of Buchan, and others. Few knew of his location. It is more likely that upon reaching Scotland, the Templars blended with those who were sympathetic to Bruce and then joined with his leaders. The Templar refugees would not have come charging into camp in their white tunics with a red cross over their left breast. They were fleeing arrest. They would come quietly, and then let Bruce know who they were and what they could do. As described in Chapter 7, Walter de Clifton testified at Holyrood that the other Templars had fled *propter scandalium exortum contra ordinem*. Also, it was said by one English Templar during his interrogation that some of the English Templars had escaped to Scotland.[3] Similarly, the French historian Raymouard stated that the Templars 'ranged themselves under the banners of Robert Bruce'.[4]

Bruce made his appearance in the late spring of 1308 when his troops were being attacked by the Earl of Buchan who was camped at Old Meldrum. Buchan was harassing both the villages in the area and Bruce and his soldiers. In response, Bruce is said to have gotten up from his sickbed and led his soldiers in an attack on Buchan. Legend has it that Bruce was still so sick that it required two other men riding along side to support him on his horse. The story concludes that the sight of 'The Bruce' in his mail was the key point in the victory. Whether Bruce was there or not, the victory, following that of Glen Trool, provided a huge boost in morale and the belief that Bruce was capable of an ultimate victory. The attack was efficient and well planned. Had the Templars begun to join Bruce's ranks? It will never be known, but the timing was right.

Aberdeen fell to Bruce in July 1308. Bruce then headed north to the land of the MacDougalls and captured Dunstaffnage Castle. In his previous battle with John MacDougall of Lorn, Bruce had been caught in an ambush and his troops had come out a poor second. But this time Bruce thwarted an ambush, and with speed and surprise he broke MacDougall's defenses. These tactics led to a number of additional victories.

Bruce's victories in the two and a half years after the spring of 1307 have been termed an astonishing reversal.[5] Bruce went from a hunted fugitive to the ruler of two-thirds of Scotland. The reversal is credited first to Bruce's brilliant leadership and tactics, and second to the Scottish Church that provided a significant amount of military intelligence. If the belief that the Templars fled to Scotland after their arrest in France is true, then there is a third reason. And this reason could well have been the cause of the rapid increase in the sophistication of Bruce's military methods.

The city of Perth fell to Bruce in January 1313. Rather than attempt a siege, Bruce's soldiers swam across the moat and scaled the castle wall using 'specially made rope-ladders'[6] – Bruce's tactics were no longer those of hit-and-run guerrilla warfare. In September 1313 the Castle of

Linlithgow fell by deception.[7] There Bruce used a hay wagon that was being taken through the gate into the town to conceal eight men. But just as the hay wagon arrived, the men jumped out and took the gate. It was a similar method to that which the Greeks were reputed to have used at the legendary siege of Troy. They held the gate until the main force arrived.

In February 1314, Sir James Douglas took Roxburgh Castle on Shrove Tuesday with sixty men disguised as cattle. After they had sneaked by the guards outside the castle, they secured their hooks and ladders, climbed the walls, opened the gates and let in the rest of Douglas's soldiers. The majority of the English force was celebrating in the great hall, and Douglas had little difficulty in taking the castle.

Bruce captured Edinburgh in March. This was done by a major diversion. Bruce had been told of a route up the steep north face. While Bruce and his forces stormed the east gate, about thirty men led by Sir Thomas Randolph climbed the north face on rope ladders. After they had scaled the castle walls it was a simple matter to open the gates. After Edinburgh was captured, the only major castle that was still in English hands was Stirling. Bruce had begun a siege on Stirling Castle, and then turned the fighting over to his brother Edward. This is the beginning for the Battle of Bannockburn.

The event that caused Scotland to become fully independent from England was Scotland's victory over England at the Battle of Bannockburn. Were the Knights Templar, in part, responsible for making victory possible for the Scots? The probability is high. The Knights Templar were in Scotland at the time of the battle because of the Pope's excommunication of Bruce. Victory over the English was essential to their ability to remain free in Scotland. They brought with them not only their fighting ability, but also their knowledge, their sources of provisions and their wealth to finance the necessary arms and armor.

The Battle of Bannockburn took place over 23–24 June 1314. But the story does not begin there. It begins a year earlier when Robert's brother Edward was holding Stirling Castle under siege, waiting for its provisions to give out. When the result seemed close, the castle's commander, Sir Philip Mowbray, had what turned out to be a brilliant idea. He offered Edward what seemed to be a way for Bruce to obtain the castle without further effort. Mowbray offered to turn the castle over to Bruce if the English had not won it back within a year, or 'If at midsummer a year thence it was not rescued by battle, he should without fail yield the castle freely.'[9]

This gave King Edward a year to prepare, and Robert the Bruce was not at all pleased. He had fought using guerrilla warfare, and battles that did not require a large number of men and arms, or well-planned logistics. But after his brother made the agreement, Bruce had to think about how to increase and better his army. As described by the chronicler John Barbour:

> That was unwisely done indeed. Never have I heard so long a warning given to so mighty a king as the King of England. For he has now in his hand England, Ireland, Wales, and Aquitaine, with all under his seignory, and a great part of Scotland, and he is so provided with treasure that he can have plenty of paid soldiers. We are few against so many. God may deal us our destiny right well, but we are set in jeopardy to lose or win all at one throw.[10]

When he learned that he had a year to amass an army against Scotland, King Edward II was elated. He proceeded to get his local affairs in order, such as settling his ongoing dispute with the Earl of Lancaster. He then began to make preparations to invade and conquer Scotland. This included raising an army that was to be from three to five times as large as the one the Scots could raise. The estimates of its size range from 20,000 to 50,000, including 2,500 heavy cavalry, 3,000 Welsh archers, and 15,000 foot soldiers. All were well appointed and well armed.[11]

In contrast, Robert the Bruce could only raise between 5,000 and 7,000 troops; they came moderately armed, but became very well trained. A rough breakdown of the sources of Bruce's soldiers includes 500 provided by Thomas Randolph, Earl of Moray, 1,000 under the command of Edward Bruce, and another 1,000 under the command of James Douglas. The largest contingent consisted of 2,000 troops under the command of Robert the Bruce.[12] All were foot soldiers. In addition, there were 500 horsemen under the command of Earl Marischal of Scotland, Sir Robert of Keith, and a small company of archers.

Even though Edward Bruce gave up the siege of Stirling Castle that he was winning, he gained several significant advantages for his brother Robert. Bruce was able to choose the field of battle. He chose the area just north of the town of Bannock. When King Edward approached Stirling, he had two choices. He could follow the old Roman road through the village of St Ninians, or attack from the plain beside the River Forth, across cultivated fields and shallow pools of water. The latter choice had obvious drawbacks. Edward decided the Roman road looked like the better choice.[13] Bannock Burn to the east was wide and dry. But King Edward was unaware of Bruce's many covered (camouflaged) holes that were from one to three feet in diameter, and up to a yard deep, that were placed throughout Bannock Burn. At the bottom of these holes were pointed caltrops to maim the horses and riders as they fell.[14] To the west of the old Roman road were Halbert's Bog and Milton Bog. Bruce had not only chosen his field of battle well, he had prepared it well.

Bruce also had the advantage of time, to prepare his army to become a well-trained force of three divisions that could each act as if it were a single entity. And he perfected the use of the schiltron, a unit that was first used by William Wallace at Falkirk. An understanding of the schiltron is essential because it was the primary method Bruce used to deploy his foot soldiers.

A schiltron is a group of trained infantry numbering from 1,000 to 2,000 soldiers. Each is equipped with a spear, usually twelve to fourteen feet long. Those at Bannockburn are said to have been twelve feet. Each foot soldier is close to the other in oval- or box-shaped phalanxes.[15] At Falkirk, the soldiers were stationary, and the spears were firmly embedded in the ground. When the English soldiers charged, the horses would become impaled on the spear, and the rider would be slain by the soldier's sword or axe. But Bruce made a significant modification to the schiltron. He caused the schiltron to be mobile. His soldiers were trained to move forward as a unit and to become offensive, rather than be a purely defensive unit.

Finally, Bruce was able to uniformly arm each of his men. Normally, a Scottish soldier brought his own armor, if any, and primitive arms, usually scythes and various types of sword. But Bruce's foot soldiers were armed with twelve-foot spears, together with a sword or axe. Each wore a steel helmet, flexible steel gloves, a back or breastplate, or a padded leather jacket.[16] These weapons and the armor cost far more than Bruce had available from the nobles that supported him. The Scottish economy was in ruins. Most of the wealthy lowland nobles supported the English, even if they had signed treaties with Bruce. The logical source of funds for the weapons and armor, and the expertise to train the thousands of troops, was the Templars.

Those who firmly believe that there were no Templars at Bannockburn uniformly point out that there are no records of their presence. But the records of the battle are so poor that it is not known where the main battle actually took place. As shown in Figure 12, there are at least four, possibly five sites for the main battle.[17] The area is very large, as can be seen from the aerial view shown in Figure 13. The best that Dr Watson and Dr Anderson, the authors of the report *The Battle of Bannockburn*, can do, using existing primary sources, is to narrow the five possible sites down to three. If this is the best that can be accomplished in terms of the location of the site on 24 July, then it is not unexpected that the existing primary sources are not written with the detail necessary to focus on what was left of a group of warriors who had fled from France and Italy to join Bruce's forces seven years before the battle.

The reports and chronicles that exist today state that from the beginning, the Battle of Bannockburn was brilliantly fought by Robert the Bruce and his leaders. The English were astounded by the well-armed, well-trained schiltrons. They were caught flat-footed and unprepared. The result was that Bruce's troops prevailed on the first day. But this did not come without cost: the English lost a significant number of men, but these men were replaceable by reason of their number. Bruce's forces were exhausted, and the foot soldiers in and out of the schiltrons had no replacements.

The second day was crucial. At the urging of Sir Alexander Seton, it started with the Scots attacking at first light.[18] In general, the battle continued as before; the English horse and foot soldiers charged against the Scottish schiltrons. But the English gained the advantage when they managed to place their archers in a position that allowed them to rain arrows down on the Scots.

History tells us that Bruce won, and won decisively. The battle was concluded by a final charge of either the cavalry under Sir Robert of Keith, or by the charge of peasants and servants (the small folk) from what has come to be known as Gillies Hill.[19] In either case, it is probable that the Knights Templar were involved. This is evident from the massive amounts of foot soldier armaments, and the individual protective wear that was available to Bruce. This was essential if the Scots were to win the battle.

In addition, even before the Battle of Bannockburn Bruce's soldiers were very well provisioned, even though Scotland was barren from twenty years of war with England, and its citizens lived in near poverty. The soldiers were provisioned for not only the battle, but for the weeks required for their training. Bruce's soldiers were trained and armed to a level never seen before or after the Battle of Bannockburn. The question is how did they accomplish this? The answer is the Templars: their knowledge, their skill and their wealth. This may have been the result of the hypothetical agreement made during the Scottish inquisition between Walter de Clifton and Bishop Lamberton, that the Templars would provide Bruce with arms, money and expertise, and the Templars could have sanctuary in Scotland.[20] But the facts and circumstances indicate that Bruce was already giving the Templars sanctuary and receiving Templar help. This would make such an agreement unnecessary.

There were numerous battles, many using battle formations other than schiltrons, significant heroism, and many stories that can be told about what occurred during the Battle of Bannockburn. They are described in detail in the books that survey Scottish history or biographies of Robert the Bruce. What is significant here is the question of what decided the battle? Granted, each of Bruce's leaders performed brilliantly. But the circumstances lead to the conclusion that it was the foresight of Bruce, and the help of the Templars and Robert of Keith's cavalry, that decided the battle.

The first turning point in the battle occurred when King Edward was able to flank Bruce's soldiers with his archers. King Edward had a special body of archers. When they were in position to assault Bruce's schiltrons, their arrows were so numerous they inflicted severe injuries on Bruce's forces. But Bruce was not without a solution: Sir Robert of Keith's 500 mounted, well-armed knights and men-at-arms on light horses. They had been purposefully held back by Bruce. In order to diminish the effectiveness of the archers, Bruce sent the cavalry into their ranks and attacked them with spears. The charge was successful. Keith's cavalry was so fierce that the whole body of archers broke and fled. Many of them retreated back into the English ranks, only to be beaten up by the other English soldiers.[21] This was followed by the charge of the 'small folk' from Gillies Hill. When King Edward saw all of this he attempted to flee to Stirling Castle. He was told he would not be admitted so he hid, and then quietly made his way back to London.

In the context of the Bannockburn/Knights Templar legend, much of what has been written about the battle involves what came to be known as the small folk behind Gillies Hill. For this reason, their involvement deserves a more detailed discussion. The small folk are described as a motley group of servants and camp followers who made up a barely armed militia that were stiffened by clansmen from the west, mainly the Robertsons under their chief, Duncan Reamhair. During the battle they hid in a valley behind Gillies Hill. In total they may have numbered 2,000.[22]

There are two major versions of the story of the charge from Gillies Hill. One begins when Edward's banner was seen leaving the field. Then 'yeomen, swains, and camp-followers', joining together as a body, elected one of them as captain and vowed to help their lords to the utmost. They then fastened broad sheets for banners and hoisted them on long poles and spears. When they came to a place where they could see the battle, they gave a shout: 'Upon them! On them boldly!'[23] And then they charged. To the English, they were seen as a new, fresh company of soldiers that were as great in number as those they were fighting.

Another version is that the soldiers behind Gillies Hill were Bruce's own brigade, largely composed of highlanders and islanders from the west coast under Angus Og Macdonald of Islay. They had been waiting for hours, and when Bruce gave the order they entered the field with a loud and swift highland charge. Their vigor and energy is said to have turned the tide of the battle.[24] This gave Bruce's troops new motivation, and created panic in the English troops who fled back into their own brigades, who in turn fled.

A very good description of the result is found in *Robert Bruce: King of Scots*, by Nina Brown Baker,

Seeing the King in flight, the English lost what little heart they had. Their demoralization was completed by a new hoard of men who burst yelling out of the woods. These were the 'gillies,' or servants, a motley crowd of hostlers and cooks who had been left in the camp. They had blackened their faces with soot, snatched up their shovels and pitchforks, and came of their own will to join the fight. To the superstitious English soldiers, already far gone in panic, they were visible devils from hell, let loose by their infernal master. The panic became a rout and hundreds were crushed and trampled in the wild flight that ended a day of honor and of glory. (24 June 1314).[25]

But would the seasoned English knights and warriors be fooled by a bunch of disorganized servants or 'undisciplined rabble'?[26] There had to be something else that would strike fear in the English troops. The logical answer is that the core of the hoard of men was made up of knights. But all the knights that fought for Bruce had been fighting with him since the beginning of the battle. There were no other knights available, unless Bruce had a group that he held back. The popular legend is that the substance of the force coming over Gillies Hill were Knights Templar in their white tunics with the red Templar cross. Their reputation was well known to the English. One does not have to think long or hard to realize that the sight of the white tunics could cause panic among the English troops. But the Templars had been fighting in northern Scotland for up to seven years. It seems a stretch to think that, without the likes of Louis Vuitton luggage, a Templar's linen tunic would have survived. There is also the strong opinion that 'the English would have broken and fled, even if the charge had not taken place'.[27]

The question then becomes, did the Knights Templar take part in the battle at all? They may not have. But if they did, did they make up part of Sir Robert of Keith's cavalry? Were they at the front of it? This battle has been described as decisive.[28] The Knights Templar had been highly proficient warriors. But they were also arrogant and would not have been inclined to mix with undisciplined rabble. They would not sit behind a hill during a two-day battle and do nothing. Being among the world's greatest horsemen, the Knights Templar would have joined with the cavalry.

There is no question that the servants and watchers stormed over Gillies Hill at the end of the Battle of Bannockburn. But that is all they did. The remainder of Edward II's forces may have panicked and fled, but the retreat and flight had already begun. The Battle of Bannockburn had been won, and the circumstances compel the conclusion that the Knights Templar, with Sir Robert of Keith's cavalry, affected the *coup de grace*. The surge of people behind Gillies Hill provided the final motivation for the English to flee.

It is suggested that the involvement of the Templars at Bannockburn diminishes the achievements of Robert the Bruce by implying that victory was only possible with the Templars' outside help.[29] But this view overlooks the qualities of an unquestionably great leader who focused on what was necessary to win. In this context, there is no question that Robert the Bruce would have used every advantage available to enable his vastly outnumbered and under-armed forces to achieve victory. And, it was Robert the Bruce who provided the unparalleled leadership to bring all of the elements together.

NOTES

1 Reconstructed by Dr Ian MacLeod, a consultant at the Edinburgh Dental Institute, and Dr Richard Neave, one of Britain's foremost forensic medical artists.

2 Sadler, John, *Scottish Battles, From Mons Graupius to Culloden*, Canongate Books, Ltd (Edinburgh, 1996), p. 45.

3 Baigent, Michael and Leigh, Richard, *The Temple and the Lodge*, Arcade Publishing (New York, 1989), p. 65.

4 Burnes, James, *Sketch of the History of the Knights Templar*, Wm. Blackwood & Sons (Edinburgh, 1849), p. 60.

5 Scott, Robert McNair, *Robert the Bruce, King of Scots*, Carroll & Graf Publishers (New York, 1996), p. 116.

6 Magnusson, Magnus, *Scotland: The Story of a Nation*, Atlantic Monthly Press (New York, 2000), p. 180.

7 Sadler, *Scottish Battles*, p. 46.

8 This discussion is not, and does not attempt to be, a thorough discussion of what happened at the Battle of Bannockburn. For this the reader is directed to *The Battle of Bannockburn*, A Report for Stirling Council, by Dr. Fiona Watson and Dr. Maggie Anderson, (Viewforth, Stirling, May, 2001), and its extensive Bibliography.

9 Barbour, John, *The Brus*, compiled 1375, translated by George Eyre-Todd, Gowans & Grey Limited (Glasgow, 1907), p. 182.

10 Ibid., p. 184.

11 Scott, *Robert the Bruce*, p. 145.

12 Ibid., pp. 146–147.

13 Maxwell, Sir Herbert, Bart. M.P., *Robert the Bruce and the Struggle for Scottish Independence*, 2nd edn, G.P. Putnam & Son, The Knickerbocker Press (New York, 1897), pp. 200–201.

14 A caltrop is a device with four metal points so arranged so that when three are lying flat on the ground, the fourth projects up. Small ones are a hazard to the hoofs of horses. The prong of a big one will pierce a horse or man as they fall.

15 Magnusson, *Scotland*, p. 142.

16 Scott, *Robert the Bruce*, p. 147.

17 Watson, Fiona and Anderson, Maggie, *The Battle of Bannockburn*, A Report for Stirling Council (Viewforth, Stirling, May 2001).

18 Barrow, G.W.S., *Robert Bruce*, University of California Press (Berkeley & Los Angeles, 1965), p. 310.

19 The original name of the hill is Coxet Hill. But, with the story of the 'small folk', the name is now generally known as Gillies Hill.

20 The full theory appears to have been first published by Archie McKerracher in 'Bruce's Secret Weapon', *The Scots Magazine* (June 1991), pp. 261, 265.

In his article, Mr McKerracher argues that 'In January 1309 Edward II of England ordered Sir John Segrave, his appointed Guardian of Scotland, to arrest all of the Templars who were still at large in Scotland and report them to the Inquisitor's Deputy, William Lamberton, Bishop of St. Andrew. Bishop Lamberton had been released from Winchester Castle the year before, had taken a new oath of allegiance to Edward II, and had gone directly to Rome for visit with the Pope.

'When he arrived in Scotland, the "wily Lamberton" paid lip service to the Pope's edicts and the English king's instructions, but remained totally committed to the cause of the excommunicated Robert the Bruce and Scottish independence.'

In December 1309, Lamberton summoned two Templar Knights to Holyrood. It's not known precisely what was discussed, but historians have made a good guess. Instead of interrogating them, it is more likely that Lamberton made an offer. 'Supply us with arms, money and expertise, and we will give the Templars sanctuary in Scotland where the Pope's writ does not run.' Because of conditions in Scotland the papal bulls were never proclaimed there, and legally, the Templars were never dissolved.

From that time on the fortunes of Robert the Bruce took a dramatic turn for the better. War materiel began arriving in Scotland from Ireland in considerable quantity. This so alarmed the English that Edward II issued an edict in 1310 to his officials in Ireland, 'prohibiting under the highest penalties all the exportation of provisions, horses, amour, and other supplies from ports where any vessel touches ... to the insurgent Scots – which he hears is carried by merchants in Ireland.'

There was, however, no arms industry in that impoverished country, and the principal towns such as Dublin were in English hands, so where were all these weapons coming from?

Only the Knights Templar had access to such large quantities of armaments and they had extensive holdings in Ireland, including at least six preceptories and eleven castles. Although some of the Irish Templars were arrested in 1308, the rest seem to have moved to the Order's properties throughout the country.

When the authorities later burst into the Irish Templar properties they found them empty of weapons, and as the historian H. Wood remarks in his tract 'The Templars in Ireland': 'It is extremely surprising to find the abodes of a military order so poorly equipped with arms.' This was about the same period as Edward was complaining about the export of arms to Scotland. Thus, there seems little doubt it was Templar arms that were being shipped to Scotland in Templar ships.

This description has often been repeated, with slight modifications – first by Mr McKerracher in 'Who Won at Bannockburn?' *The Highlander* (July/August 1994), pp. 62–83. It then appeared in *Stone of Destiny*, Canongate Books Ltd (Edinburgh, 1997), p. 130, by Pat Gerber. It was then mentioned by Michael, HRH Prince of Albany, in *The Forgotten Monarchy of Scotland*, Element (Shaftesbury, Dorset, 1998), p. 64. Recently, in the May/June issue of *The Highlander*, pp. 40–41, it again appeared in an article by Bowen Pearse, 'Were the Knights Templar at the Battle at Bannockburn?'

The last article was rebutted by Lin Robinson's article 'The Knights Templar at Bannockburn – A Rebuttal', *The Highlander* (September/October 2008). The article points out the fact that the inventories after the Templar arrests showed little 'treasure, cash, gold and silver'. But this would be consistent with its removal prior to 13 October. It is then said 'That the myth says that Scotland was poor and militarily weak in 1314. This is not true.' In fact, with constant warfare, the Scottish people were poor and could barely generate enough crops and raise enough animals to live on. But the Scots, after 1307, were never militarily weak. And it is very possible that between 1311 and 1314 Robert the Bruce received 'in excess of £40,000'. But this is only £6.66 to feed and arm, for several months, each of 6,000 soldiers. Today, £6.66 has a buying power of £175 per soldier. And it also assumes that there is no other use for the money. In terms of the battle, the author overlooks the fact that on 24 July Bruce's troops were exhausted. Several accounts state that up until King Edward II brought out the archers, the battle was close to a draw, with the advantage to the English. It was not until the light cavalry of Sir Robert Keith that the battle turned in favor of the Scots. Next the author points out that none of the accounts of the battle refer to the Templars. But as stated in the main text, there were no investigative reporters in 1314. As described in the appendix, the Templars in Scotland would have been late middle-aged advisors. They wanted safety and would not have come in wearing their habit and flying their banners. The article then goes on to discuss the possibility that the Templars could not have brought tactics learned from the Saracens. This is not necessarily correct because even though none of the Templars who came to Scotland had *fought* in Outremer, many of them had trained there. And it is known that Bruce's battle plans went from guerilla warfare to sophisticated tactics very quickly, and in line with the time the Templars would have come to Scotland.

Mr McKerracher's argument seems unnecessary. The Templars, their treasure and their ships left France in late September/early October 1307. Bruce's victories began in the spring of 1308. By December 1309, the Templars were already in Scotland. Why wait and make a deal with an intermediary? The Templars were arrogant knights and would have dealt directly with Robert the Bruce. The documents referred to by Mr McKerracher may record an agreement between Bishop Lamberton and Walter de Clifton, but it is more than likely that the agreement, if it existed, simply reiterated existing facts.

21 Barrow, *Robert Bruce*, p. 325.

22 Ibid., pp. 46–47.

23 Barbour, *The Brus*, pp. 222–223.

24 Magnusson, *Scotland*, p. 185. Unfortunately, there is no footnote or reference to support this version of the story.

25 Baker, Nina Brown, *Robert Bruce: King of Scots*, Vangard Press (New York, 1948), pp. 204–205.

26 Barrow, *Robert Bruce*, pp. 326–327.

27 Morris, John E., *Bannockburn*, University Press (Cambridge, 1914), p. 90.

28 Maxwell, *Robert the Bruce*, p. 217.

29 Lord, Evelyn, *The Knights Templar in Britain*, Pearson Education Limited (Edinburgh, 2002), p. 154.

9

ROSSLYN CHAPEL:
A TEMPLAR LEGACY?

Is Rosslyn Chapel really just a collegiate chapel, or is it a repository of the secrets and treasure of the Knights Templar?

India may have the Taj Mahal, but Scotland has Rosslyn Chapel. Both are unique. Both are exquisite. But the purpose of the Taj Mahal is well known. It was built as a mausoleum for the emperor's favorite wife. It has no hidden purpose. The same cannot be said for Rosslyn Chapel (see Figure 13). Its interior is beautiful (Figure 14). One cannot go into Rosslyn Chapel without being overwhelmed by the experience. The carvings on the pillars, and the faces carved on the corbels, all cry out for an explanation that is far more than what is printed in the brochures.

Rosslyn Chapel is located just outside the small town of Roslin, about seven miles south of Edinburgh. It is a small, collegiate chapel located on the left bank of the North Esk River. It is one of approximately forty secular collegiate churches built in Scotland between 1248 and 1546. The reference to a 'secular church' may seem to be an oxymoron, but it is not. It is secular because it was constructed and privately owned by a family, and not by a church organization for the benefit of the public. It was a collegiate church because it was intended to have at least two pastors.

The word 'Rosslyn' is a combination of the two Gaelic words 'ros' (peninsula or promontory) and 'lynn' (waterfall), and translates to be 'Waterfall Point'. Rosslyn Chapel was built near the Saint Clair's current Rosslyn Castle, which is located on a promontory surrounded on three sides by the Esk River. Rosslyn Chapel was the Saint Clairs' second chapel, and was built where the Saint Clairs' first castle was located. It was begun on St Mathew's Day in 1446 by Sir William St Clair, the third and last St Clair Prince of Orkney, and was dedicated in 1450. In terms of theories about the history and purpose of Rosslyn Chapel, there is one for virtually every aspect of the chapel. There are several beliefs concerning the shape of the chapel. Many compare it with the Temple of Solomon that was built on the Temple Mount in Jerusalem. And there is the question of whether William St Clair ever intended to build an entire chapel, or did he only mean to build the choir, baptistery, lower chapel and underground vaults that exist today? There are also numerous understandings about the carvings. Some create questions which can never be answered to everyone's satisfaction. There is simply not enough information.

Did William St Clair intend to build a church or a chapel? The full shape of the foundation was discovered in the eighteenth century. It is a common ecclesiastical shape with a cruciform configuration, a tower at the center, transepts, a nave, all built out on an east–west axis. Because the shape of the full foundation is known, it might be said that William St Clair was confident the entire chapel would be completed. But it was not. Instead, for the next thirty-six years, William St Clair concentrated on the carvings and masonry inside the chapel.

Another point of view is that William St Clair could not match the other churches in terms of size, so he planned to surpass them in design and decoration. This theory is based on a statement of the Saint Clairs' biographer, Father Richard Augustine Hay, that the builder decided the church must be 'a most curious worke'.[1] But this overlooks the fact that the Saint Clairs were very wealthy and could have completed the entire chapel. When Sir William St Clair died in 1484, the four walls and the carved interior were complete. The nave, transepts and tower had not been started. The designs for the roof had been approved, but not begun. In terms of funding, Sir William endowed the use of the chapel with funds for a provost, six prebendaries and two choristers.[2] But he provided no funds for further construction. His son, Sir Oliver St Clair, finished the roof, but left most of the chapel incomplete.[3] The only part of the chapel that was complete was the choir.

If Rosslyn Chapel is a secular, collegiate chapel, with no relation to the Knights Templar, it was built by William for two basic purposes: for saying prayers for the souls of the past and present Saint Clair family, and as a permanent place of burial for family members.

For several hundred years these were the purposes of Rosslyn Chapel. The family held services to pray for the souls of the living and departed Saint Clairs. Members of the family were buried in the chapel's vault. If the chapel was to be used for any other purpose, there are, unfortunately, no surviving original designs or notes. Based on what does survive, it would seem the chapel was ultimately intended to be what it was, a collegiate family chapel, and nothing more. But, the absence of any original designs or notes, together with its numerous enigmatic carvings, have allowed for the creation of numerous claims, suppositions and theories which have, by themselves, created and added to the chapel's mystique.

With all that has been written about the Templars and Rosslyn Chapel, there is no mention of the fact the Templars did not require the use of Rosslyn Chapel until after 1534, when James Sandilands relinquished Balantrodoch, along with other Templar and Hospitaller properties, to Queen Mary. Until then, the Templars would have had the use of the chapel they had built in the late twelfth century at Balantrodoch, which is only a short distance away from Rosslyn Chapel. But by 1534 the Templars, who had been formally dissolved for 222 years, were no longer a separate organized fighting force, and no longer possessed immense wealth. Their activities consisted of such things as passing along Templar traditions, conducting ceremonies and managing their properties. Because the chapel was finished or completed in 1546, there would have been only twelve years when the Templars were without a chapel, and Rosslyn Chapel was under construction. This is a very short time for any major contributions by the Templars. And, in fact, the chapel had been essentially complete forty years after it was begun. So during these twelve years probably nothing new was created.

As a result of the Reformation and its prohibitions, Rosslyn Chapel was not used as a chapel from 1592 through 1736.[4] As a result, in 1592 Oliver St Clair was forbidden from burying his wife there. It was not used again as a church until 1738 when James St Clair began restoration by repairing the roof and installing a new flagstone floor. Sunday services did not take place again until 1861, when they were begun by the third Earl of Rosslyn who also undertook further restoration work,

which was possible because even though the chapel had been periodically ransacked, it had been kept locked for a great deal of the time.[5]

Was the chapel built with the help or guidance of the Knights
Templar? Is there a treasure, or sacred papers, or the Holy Grail, or the
Ark of the Covenant hidden in the vaults under Rosslyn Chapel? There
are two clear-cut views. One is that Sir William created a storehouse of
secret coded Templar information, a legacy to those who seek spiritual
enlightenment; that the interior of the chapel is a veritable, three-
dimensional 'teaching board' of gnostic, late medieval initiation.[6] This
view is supported by the interpretation of many of the chapel's carvings, and a grave slab in the chapel with the name of William St Clair
(see Figure 15). The slab is about 40 inches long by 11.75 inches wide
by 6 inches thick. It has been reused and the letters have been re-cut. It
sits on a plinth or base that is said to be modern, and cannot be dated.
The name on the slab has the carving 'WILL★HMDES★HINCLER' or
'William Sinclair'. The carving on the plinth is:

WILLIAM DE ST. CLAIR
KNIGHT TEMPLAR

This grave slab and plinth are said to be proof of the connection
between the Knights Templar and Rosslyn Chapel. This is where the
bones of William St Clair, who fought at Bannock and died in Spain
fighting the Moors with Sir James Douglas while taking Robert the
Bruce's heart to the Holy Land, are said to be buried. The bones would
have been brought back to Scotland by Sir William Keith of Galston
who had been prominent in Bruce's taking of Berwick in 1318, and
who was one of the few who survived in Spain.[7] The problem is that
there is little or no evidence of what happened to the bones, or even if
they were brought back from Spain. But if they were, it is not difficult
to posit that Sir William's bones were first buried by the Saint Clairs
near Rosslyn Castle, possibly in the graveyard of the Saint Clairs' first
collegiate church of St Mathew.[8] They were then simply reburied in
Rosslyn Chapel to commemorate his involvement with Robert the
Bruce and Bannockburn, rather than having his remains secreted in
a closed underground vault. Also, if this William St Clair became the
Scottish Master of the Order, this would explain the small gravestone,
which is normally used for a child, and the fact that the skull was

placed over the crossed femurs.[9] The small space beneath the small tombstone would be all that was necessary for the skeletal remains.[10]

The counter-argument has been succinctly stated by Karen Ralls, the author of two books on the Knights Templar, who worked for four years at Rosslyn Chapel as the deputy director of the Rosslyn Chapel Museum Exhibition. Simply put, her argument is that the chapel's founder, Sir William St Clair, was not a Templar, because the Order had been officially dissolved in 1312, and the foundation stone for Rosslyn was not laid until work began in 1446, some 134 years later. Ideas that Rosslyn Chapel was a possible repository for many artifacts, including the lost Scrolls of the Temple, the Ark of the Covenant, the Holy Grail, and the genuine stone of destiny, are all theories that remain speculation.[11] But when there are no records or 'notes', and because of the paucity of archival records of the Templars, it is difficult to establish that Templar involvement did not exist.[12]

Those who believe that the Knights Templar continued to exist in Scotland after their arrest and dissolution, tend to accept the traditions that the Saint Clair heirs and the Knights Templar used a hidden room under the chapel as an initiation chamber, and that the vaults beneath the chapel contain something other than crypts.[13] Whether the traditions are true is an impossible question to answer because the Sinclair family will not open the vault. The closest anyone has come to examining the vault's interior occurred when Andrew Sinclair was allowed to use the latest radar technique developed for modern archaeology, called a Groundscan, to survey the whole chapel.[14] The machine has the ability to detect shapes and metal objects through stone and rubble. He reports that large cavities, i.e. vaults, were found below the chapel. He also detected reflectors, which indicated metal, probably the armor of the buried knights. There was also a large reflector under the Lady Chapel which suggested the presence of a metallic shrine. But there was no evidence of what could be described as gold or silver 'treasure'.[15]

There are two significant pillars in the Rosslyn Chapel, the Apprentice Pillar and the Mason's Pillar. Advocates of Templar involvement suggest that these two pillars represent the two pillars of Boaz and Jachin, which stood at the inner hallway of Solomon's Temple in Jerusalem above the catacombs where the Templars spent their first nine years.[16] Of particular significance is the Apprentice Pillar, which may have been created to enclose the Holy Grail, or the chalice from which Jesus of Nazareth and his disciples drank wine at the Last Supper. To many, the Holy Grail has become a Templar relic. If it was brought to Scotland after the Templar suppression, it might have been left with the Saint Clairs.[17]

The Apprentice Pillar is one of three at the head of the choir. The story of the Apprentice Pillar tells much of the chapel's mystique. The master mason who was given the commission to carve the pillar was given a model. The model was of such exquisite design that the mason was not sure if he could carry out the work. To insure his ability to carve the pillar, he traveled to Rome to view and examine the original. While he was away, his apprentice had a vision of the magnificent finished pillar and immediately began carving the pillar. The result is what is seen today. When the master mason returned he could not believe what he saw, and was awed by the workmanship in the finished pillar. When he asked who carved the pillar, he was told that it had been carved by his apprentice. As the story goes, the master mason was both envious and furious. In a rage he struck the apprentice on the head with his mallet, killing him. Those who believe the chalice on the St Clair tombstone is the Holy Grail believe that the Grail is hidden within the Apprentice Pillar, and that this pillar was created to enclose it. But Andrew Sinclair scanned the Apprentice Pillar with the Groundscan. There was no evidence of a gold or silver chalice inside it.[18]

A carving of the apprentice's head, with an indentation at the top of his right forehead, is one of the carvings inside Rosslyn Chapel.[19] The apprentice's face does not look down on the pillar of his creation but, surprisingly, on the beautiful Mason's Pillar, the third of the three, which was carved by the master mason who killed him. The Mason's Pillar is a beautifully crafted work on its own, and should not be over-looked because of the reputation or design of the Apprentice Pillar. Of the three pillars, the middle pillar's design is generally consistent with the others in the chapel, and is called the Fellow Craft Pillar.

The carving of the Agnus Dei (Lamb of God) in Rosslyn Chapel is a key Christian symbol that occurs in a number of Templar build-ings on the continent. It also occurs on the seals of various Templar Masters. As a result, this may be a possible Templar connection. But this symbol also occurs in many other medieval non-Templar churches and church buildings. It has long been an important Christian symbol of martyrdom, so it is not particularly unique to Rosslyn Chapel or the Templars.

One of the corbels[20] in a window in the south aisle has a carving of a knight riding a horse, with a figure behind the hindquarters of the horse holding a 'passion' cross (see Figure 16). The second figure does not appear to be mounted. It has been claimed that this carving represents the seal of the Templars.[21] If it is, then this carving could be a connecting link. But the seal has two riders on one horse, symbolic of the Templars' early poverty. If the carving is not the Templar seal, the question remains, what does it depict? There are at least three views:

The first view directly involves the Knights Templar. It describes a mailed Templar knight with his lance. Behind the knight's saddle is an angel, carrying the Cross of the Church militant.[22] The angel is there to protect the Templar whose calling was to fight and defeat the Saracens in Outremer.

The second view describes the carving of a mounted knight as being St George slaying the dragon. The second figure is an angel bearing a crucifix. The dragon is absent because the lower part of the carving, including the lower limbs of the horse, is missing. But the direction of the spear indicates that something should be there, and that could be the dragon.[23]

The third view is that it depicts William the Seemly St Clair as he escorts Princess Margaret to marry King Malcolm Canmore of Scotland.[24] The cross she is carrying is said to be the Holy Rood, or a portion of the 'true cross' upon which Jesus was crucified. Because this event occurred in 1094, it could not possibly involve the Templars.

A carving in Rosslyn Chapel's retro choir is said to be the carving of the death mask of Robert the Bruce. There is a belief that Robert the Bruce was not only a Templar, but that he was the sovereign Grand Master of the Templars, and that his death mask is carved into the stonework at Rosslyn. But there is no known death mask of Robert the Bruce, let alone one that survived for 117 years. Also, the creation of a death mask was a major event. A death mask of Bruce would have been an important artifact, and prominently displayed anywhere in Scotland.

The idea of Bruce's death mask may have begun with Andrew Sinclair's *The Sword and the Grail* at plate 10, between pp. 150–151, where he described the image as the 'Supposed death mask of Robert the Bruce'. But he does not attempt to expand on this supposition and there is nothing in the book that supports it. The carving looks more like a peasant with a peasant's hat. Further, the carving is in no way alike to the forensic reconstruction of Bruce's head (see Figure 11). Robert the Bruce's grave was found in 1818 in Dunfermline Abbey. Dr Ian MacLeod, a consultant at the Edinburgh Dental Institute, and Dr Richard Neave, a forensic medical artist, produced a reconstruction of Bruce's head. Dr MacLeod describes Bruce, with his battle scars and possible leprosy:

> The first thing that strikes you about Robert the Bruce is that the guy has tremendous presence. There is almost a Churchillian aura about him. This was a guy you would not want to get into a fight with. He would have stood out from the crowd. What we have here is a battle-scarred old man. You don't go through wars like he did without receiving a few knocks.[25]

There is also a carving of a heart held by an angel that is said to be the heart of Robert the Bruce. More likely, the angel is holding a cushion on which lies the shape of a heart, which represents Jesus Christ. The winged figure could represent an angel, or St Mathew to whom the chapel is dedicated.[26]

Then there are the Green Men (see Figure 17). These are faces of men with foliage growing out of their mouths that are carved throughout Rosslyn Chapel. The foliage is said to represent fertility. The facial images range from young to old, from angry to happy, from that of a pixy to that of a rogue.

The association with Green Men and the Templars stems from such things as a comparison of the Green Men to the head of the Baphomet, and the existence of Green Men in Templar chapels and temples throughout Europe. The Baphomet is an ill-defined, amorphous, heathen image that the Templars were accused of worshipping by Philip IV. Because there is no clear definition or known image of a Baphomet, there is no bridge between it and the Green Men.[27] Images of Green Men are widespread. They have pagan origins and represent such things as fertility and abundance. They are found in Celtic ruins, and in the Far East. One of the most discussed locations for Green Men is the famed Chartres Cathedral in France which contains a number of Green Men among its carvings. The connection to the Templars is that the Templars are said to have had a significant influence in the cathedral's design. But this overlooks the fact that Green Men appear in many Christian churches and cathedrals all over Europe. As a result, the use of Green Men by the Templars does not necessarily connect Rosslyn Chapel's Green Men to the Templars.

Rosslyn Chapel abounds with mystery. Do the carvings have an independent significance, or are they purely decorative? Do they reflect the new Gnosticism that was emerging in medieval Europe? Were the Saint Clairs closely allied with the Knights Templar? Did the Saint Clairs provide a safe harbor to the Templars who had escaped from France just before their arrest in 1307? Did the Saint Clairs provide a place from which new Templars could be recruited and trained? It should not be forgotten that the Templars' original land grant at Balantrodoch was said to originally have been owned by the Saint Clairs. With the proximity of Balantrodoch to Rosslyn Chapel there must have been constant interaction in Scotland between the Templars and the Saint Clairs. Did this interaction continue after the arrests in 1307 and the Templars' dissolution in 1312?

The existing known evidence about Rosslyn Chapel and the Knights Templar points to a conclusion that they were not directly connected. The chapel was built to be a small, unique collegiate chapel. Its carvings are symbolic of the times and Christianity. The vaults were crypts for the Saint Clair family. The pillars are simply ornate. Arguably, the grave slab and plinth are recent, possibly added by the Freemasons in their efforts to link the Knights Templar directly with their Order in the early nineteenth century in line with the efforts of Alexander Deuchar.

Yet there is a strong argument that the Templars existed in Scotland from 1307 through to the present time. And even if none of the Saint Clairs were actually members of the Order, they undoubtedly had a close working relationship. Consequently, a connection between Rosslyn Chapel and the Templars cannot be dismissed.

Today, Rosslyn Chapel is used extensively by numerous Templar Orders, including those based in Scotland and Europe. In 1997 an investiture by the Grand Priory of the Scots was filmed by cable television's The History Channel as part of its episode *In Search of History: The Knights Templar.*[28]

In 2005 I participated in a Templar investiture at Rosslyn Chapel that was held by the international Templar Order, *Ordo Supremus Militaris Templi Hierosolymitani.* Templar Knights from Scotland, England, France and the United States were present. The mystique that existed in 2005 was as great as it would have been in the fifteenth century. Today's Templar ceremonies are much like they were 800 years ago. As knights, we were garbed in our white Templar mantles with the red Templar cross over the left breast. The chaplain said prayers that originated with the Templars 800 years ago. Hearing the prayers and watching the ceremonies in 2005, I absolutely lost my place in time. I forgot that I was in the year 2005, and that Rosslyn Chapel is operated by The Rosslyn Trust, and that the chapel is not only available to the Templars, but to any other group. During the Templar ceremony, there existed a feeling of awe that was overpowering. If you had asked me then if I believed Rosslyn Chapel was built for and by the Knights Templar, my answer would have been unequivocally – yes!

But that is why so many seek to find a direct connection to the Templars.

NOTES

1   Cooper, Robert L.D., *The Rosslyn Hoax? Viewing Rosslyn Chapel from a new perspective*, Lewis (UK, 2006), p. 105, citing *The Genealogie of the Sainteclairs of Rosslyn*, ed. Cooper, Robert L.D., The Grand Lodge of Scotland (2002), pp. 26–27.

2   www.rosslynchapel.com/history/history-pt2.htm

3   Wallace-Murphy, Tim & Hopkins, Marilyn, *Rosslyn, Guardian of the Secrets of the Holy Grail*, Element Books Limited (Shaftesbury, Dorset, 1999), pp. 8–9.

4   www.rosslynchapel.com/history/history-pt2.htm

5   Ibid.

6   Wallace-Murphy, *Rosslyn*, p. 107.

7   Sinclair, Andrew, *The Sword and the Grail*, Birlinn Limited (Edinburgh, 2002), p. 3.

8   Ibid.

9   Ibid.

10 Ibid.

11 Ralls, Karen, *Knights Templar Encyclopedia*, New Page Books (Franklin Lakes, 2007), pp. 157–159.

12 In *The Rosslyn Hoax?* Mr Cooper devotes much of the work to an effort to dispel the Templar myths surrounding Rosslyn Chapel.

13 Wallace-Murphy, *Rosslyn*, p. 127.

14 As of this writing, John Ritchie, the Grand Herald, then the press spokes-man for the *Militi Templi Scotia*, was planning to conduct ground scans of Rosslyn Chapel's vaults and the surrounding area.

15 Sinclair, *The Sword and the Grail*, p. 86.

16 Ibid., p. 83.

17 Ibid., p. 76.

18 Ibid., p. 86.

19 The scar may be a relatively recent addition. Cooper, *The Rosslyn Hoax?* p. 145.

20 A stone bracket that supports a cornice or overhang.

21 Cooper, *The Rosslyn Hoax?* p. 155.

22 Sinclair, *The Sword and the Grail*, p. 105.

23 Cooper, *The Rosslyn Hoax?* pp. 155–156.

24 Wallace-Murphy, *Rosslyn*, p. 199.

25 Cooper, *The Rosslyn Hoax*, p. 152.

26 Ibid., p. 153.

27 The Baphomet has been described as a head worshipped in secret by the Templars, a human head that was half-gold or half-silver, or half-shaven or half-unshaven, the embalmed head of Jesus Christ. It is also described as an old French corruption of Muhammad. The most imaginative definition is by Hugh Shonfield in *The Essene Oddessey*, Element (Dorset, 1993), who applies an Essene cipher to obtain the name Sophia, the goddess of wisdom.

28 'In Search of History: The Knights Templar', © 1997 A & E Television Networks.

10

THE TEMPLARS AFTER BANNOCKBURN

The modern Scottish Knights Templar would have begun in 1309 with Walter de Clifton, the Preceptor of Scotland, who, after the Templar inquisition, would have become the Grand Master of Scotland.[1] The Templar inquisition in Scotland only extended north to Edinburgh and Stirling Castle, the area controlled by Edward II. Robert the Bruce controlled most of the remainder of Scotland. But in the eyes of Edward II, Bruce was simply 'a proscribed fugitive' and Edward had to do everything possible to assert what authority he had. That changed after the Battle of Bannockburn. And, after Bannockburn, each successive Bruce and Stewart king is said to have been a Knight Templar.[2] In addition, after Bannockburn Robert the Bruce confirmed all prior grants of both Templar and Hospitaller property. This process of confirmation is said to have been continued by Bruce's successors.[3]

After Bannockburn, the direct evidence of the Templars' presence in Scotland is sparse and anecdotal. But this must be viewed in conjunction with the fact that during the fourteenth and fifteenth centuries the Templars continued to control a considerable amount of property. Much of it was leased to tenants for a fixed rent, or man-service, or both. Other properties were managed by the baillis described in Chapter 3. Taken together, with the continued existence of the Templars' lands and estates, and the events that periodically occurred, there appears to be a sufficient amount of circumstantial evidence to support an argument for the continued existence of the Templars in Scotland after the Battle of Bannockburn, through the twentieth century to the present.

In addition, there are two separate facts that support the survival of the Templars. While there is clear evidence that title to the Templar lands was eventually transferred to the Hospitallers, there is no record that the Hospitallers replaced the Templar baillis. Further, an arrangement between the Templars and Hospitallers was both natural and politic. In Scotland the Templars independently possessed property. But even though the Templars continued to exist in Europe, the ban against the Templars also remained. The result was that the Templars' ability to conduct business was severely constricted. On the other hand, the Hospitallers, who also possessed significant influence and wealth, were well received by the continental sovereigns. This permitted the Templars to be represented before the courts in Europe.[4] The other fact is that both Orders were represented in the Scottish Parliament by the Preceptor of the Order of St John.[5]

Between 1307 and 1314, the Templars' activities in Scotland would have continued as they had before the arrests in France by Philip IV. Pope Clement V's second papal bull *Ad providam*, which transferred the Templars' property to the Hospitallers, was ignored in Scotland, and it was decades before the Hospitallers even attempted to obtain title and possession of the Templar property there. The reason for this was that after Bruce was crowned king and began to control much of Scotland, there were few, if any, Hospitallers who remained. The Hospitallers had had a strong English connection which made it difficult for them to remain when Bruce began to gain control of Scotland, or to return after Bannockburn. Also, unlike the Scots of that time and the Templars, the Hospitallers remained loyal to the Pope.[6]

In 1338 Brother Philip de Thame, Prior of London, reported that the lands of the Hospitallers in Scotland, and the 'lands of the Templars in Scotland, are burned and brought to nothing, so that nothing can be obtained from them'.[7] What is unusual is that lands of the Hospitallers and Templars are reported separately. Clearly there was no attempt to integrate the inventories.

Ultimately, for a period of approximately 200 years, the Scottish Templar lands (*Terrae Templariae*) were owned and accounted for by the Hospitallers, or in some cases, according to historical documents, by a combined Order called 'The Order of St John and the Temple'.

Even after the Hospitallers obtained control, the properties continued to be leased to tenants, and the Temple baillis continued to collect the rents. The Temple baillis would then report back to the Prior of St John at its headquarters at Torphichen.[8] But two additional facts are certain. The Templar inventory of properties was kept separate, and the on-site management continued to be conducted by Temple baillis. The Hospitallers did not utilize the baillie system until the middle of the fifteenth century.[9] The Temple baillis even held separate courts. 'In 1513 reference is made to a Templar-baillie for that region [sheriffdom of Ayr] and in 1532 Charles Campbell held the temple courts in the burgh of Ayr in his position as bailei.'[10]

THE DEATH OF THE GOOD SIR JAMES

One of the first events that is said to have Templar involvement occurred in 1330 when a group of Scottish knights, under the command of the most devoted and famous follower of Robert the Bruce, the Good Sir James Douglas, were taking Bruce's heart to the Holy Land to lay it on the Holy Sepulchre in Jerusalem. The tiny casket which contained Bruce's heart was tied around Sir James's neck. Their route took them through Spain. On the way the Scots made a pilgrimage to Santiago de Compostella, where they took part in the first great successful battle against the Moors at Teba. But success was not to continue. On 25 March 1330 the battle near Castile was a disaster. Sir James Douglas and the majority of the Scots were killed by the Saracens. Fortunately Bruce's heart was retrieved from the battlefield and returned to Scotland with Sir James's remains.[11] The casket was interred at the Abbey of Melrose.

Several authors have included the Templars among the group of Scots that accompanied Bruce's heart. One element that supports the belief that the Templars were present in Spain was the Scots' use of a tactic perfected by the Templars in Outremer, which was named after the Templar officer known as the Turcopolier.[12] In this formation, the Scots charged in a wedge-shape unit with such ferocity that they divided the Moorish army; then separate units would charge the divided Moorish troops. This was considered a Templar innovation because it required the knights, who normally acted to gain individual valor, to act as a cohesive unit, something that in Outremer was unique to the Templars.

THE BATTLE OF HALIDON HILL

Another reference to the Knights Templar after the Battle of Bannockburn involved a knight known as Adam De Vipont and the Battle of Halidon Hill, 19 July 1333. The De Vipont family was very much involved in the Battle of Bannockburn. John Barbour in *The Brus* specifically notes that Sir William Vipont was one of 'two worthy knights who were slain at the Battle'.[13] There were several known De Viponts in the early fourteenth century; the most notable being Sir Alan De Vipont. But the name that is found in the context of the continuation of the Knights Templar is that of Adam De Vipont, in a fictional dramatic poem by Sir Walter Scott, 'The Battle of Halidon Hill'. In the poem, Adam De Vipont is a Knight Templar, a major character in the drama, who was ultimately captured by Edward III. When Adam De Vipont is brought before King Edward, the king states:

'Vipont, thy crossed shield shows against a Christian king.'

Adam de Vipont responds, 'That Christian King is warring upon Scotland. I was a Scotsman ere I was a Templar. Sworn to my country ere I knew my Order.'

There are some that contend that this reference confirms the fact the Templars continued to fight for Scotland after the suppression of the Order in France.[14] The proposition is not without some degree of foundation. Sir Walter Scott was a friend of Alexander Deuchar who resurrected the *Militi Templi Scotia* in the early nineteenth century. In 1823 Mr Deuchar even asked Sir Walter Scott to be the Order's Grand Master, a request Sir Walter declined because of health reasons. Sir Walter Scott wrote about the Knights Templar in other works, and from his writings it is clear that he had conducted a significant amount of independent research. If this is the case, it also evidences the fact that the elder Templars who fled the inquisition did some recruiting, and that the Order did not cease to exist after the Battle of Bannockburn.

THE TEMPLARS BETWEEN 1333 AND 1488

Two examples of the discrete disposition of the Templars and the Hospitallers are found in a charter by William de Lisours the elder, dated at or about 1340, well after the dissolution of the Templars and

Bannockburn. Then about 100 years later there is a follow-up charter by a subsequent William de Lisours. Each of the two charters indicates that the Templars were separate and distinct from the Hospitallers until the middle of the sixteenth century.

There is no question that the ultimate management responsibility for the Templar estates and properties was with the Hospitallers. This is evidenced by an order given by Philibert de Naillac, Grand Master of the Hospitallers, as the result of an assembly in Avignon regarding an argument between John Binning, Thomas Goodwin, and Alexander de Leighton, which included the dire condition of several Templar houses in Scotland.[15] The situation was reviewed by a three-member commission appointed by Philibert de Naillac. Alexander de Leighton had at least two advantages. He was the only one of the three who attended the Assembly. He had also been appointed as Preceptor of the Hospitallers in Scotland. Ultimately, the Order provided that the Church of Torphichen and certain lands of Locharis be leased to John Binning, a chaplain of the Order, at an annual rent of seventy-one gold crowns. The Church of Balantrodoch, two mills, and the estates of Hudspeth, Esperston and Utterstoun, were leased to Thomas Goodwin, chaplain, with the title of Preceptor of Balantrodoch at a rent of thirty-nine gold crowns. The rest of the property, including the Templar houses, was leased to Alexander de Leighton at a rent of 289 gold crowns.

The next recorded event occurred at the beginning of the reign of King James IV, when the Templars and the Hospitallers were shown to be separate but again combined. On 19 October 1488 King James issued a charter titled *Deo et Sancto Hospitali de Jerusalem et fratribus ejusdem Militiae Templi Salamonis*, which 'reaffirms' all the ancient rights and privileges made by his predecessors to both the Order of St John and the 'Templars'.[16] Both Orders were again formally placed under the Preceptor of the Order of St John. This document is cited by many as proof of the Templars' continued existence separate and apart from the Hospitallers. It may be. Or it may be simply a reconfirmation of Pope Clement V's original papal bull.

The relationship between the Templars and the Hospitallers remained intact and unbroken until the Reformation, and what amounts to a sophisticated embezzlement of Templar and Hospitaller property by the Hospitallers' Scottish Grand Master, Sir John Sandilands. In essence, he traded the Templar and Hospitaller property, together with 10,000 crowns, to Queen Mary in exchange for the lands which were included in a barony. The scheme began in 1541 when John Sandilands traveled to Malta and obtained a commitment from the Grand Master of the Order of St John stating he would become Master of the Scottish Order upon the death of Walter Lindsey.[17] Lindsey died in 1546 and John Sandilands became the Prior of Torphichen and the head of the Order.

The Reformation began with the Act of 1560 which prohibited all allegiances. It thus annulled the rights existing under the charter of James IV. On 22 January 1564, to comply with the Act, Sir John Sandilands, as Preceptor of Torphichen, transferred the Templar and Hospitaller properties to Queen Mary. Specifically, he resigned (relinquished) to Queen Mary the lands and baronies of 'Torphicen, Listoun, Ballentrodo, Tankertoun, Dennie, Mareculter, Stanhope, and Galtua'. To insure that the transfers were complete and all inclusive, Sandilands also added in:

> their pertinents, lying in the Sheriffdoms, of Edinburgh, Pebles, Lilitngow, Striueling, Lanerk Kincardin and Stewartry of Kirkcudbritht, and also of all annual rents, templar lands, teinds, [tenants] possessions and lands what-soever as well not named as named within the Kingdom of Scotland.[18]

To put it simply, he put the Templars and the Hospitallers out of business, both in terms of assets and income. Then, on 24 January 1564, Sir James Sandilands paid Queen Mary 10,000 crowns. In return, Queen Mary granted James Sandilands a barony to be called the Barony of Torphichen, which consisted of three estates. She further exempted him from all taxes, and from being subject to any authority except the queen and the privy council.[19] This transaction ended the Hospitallers' presence in Scotland, and caused the Templars to regroup. In response, David Seton, who had inherited his family's identification with the Templars, is said to have withdrawn his association with the Hospitaller Order of St John and taken a number of Templar Knights with him.[20] This fact is stated in a family history written in 1896 about an event that occurred *c.* 1560. The author wrote: 'When the Knights-Templar were deprived of their patrimonial interest through the instrumentality of their Grand Master Sir John Sandilands, they drew off in a body with David Seton, Grand Prior of Scotland at their head.' This description may have been written 366 years after it happened, but the author's description is consistent with Sir John Sandilands' actions. It is also consistent with the Sandilands family's description of the transaction and its separate reference to both the Hospitallers and the Templars.

The result is that the Templars would have come under new leadership. In order to protect the Templars' interests, David Seton may also have reconstituted the Templars under a new name, the Order of the Knights Templar of St Anthony, with David Seton, nephew of George Lord Seton, as their Grand Master.[21] The transaction is described in a satirical poem of the period titled 'Haly Kirk and Hir Theeves', which was composed by a person who was both a Catholic and Templar, and who was repulsed by Sandilands' breach of trust (embezzlement). The last line is said to be the basis for the recognition of David Seton as the Scottish Grand Master.

> Fye upon the traitor then
> Quha has broucht us to sic pass,
> Greedie als the knave Judas!
> Fye upon the churle quhat solde
> Haly erthe for heavie golde;
> Bot the Temple felt na loss
> Quhan David Setoune bare the Crosse.[22]

Sir David Seton died abroad in 1581 and was buried in the Church of the Scottish Convent at Ratisbon, which is now Regensburg near Nuremberg.[23] After this the Templars were silent. But they continued to exist, and stayed connected with the Jacobites.[24] This becomes historically credible when viewed in the context of two separate events. One involved hospitals; the other involved the Viscount Dundee, John Graham of Claverhouse, also known as Bonnie Dundee.

THE HOSPITALS AND BONNIE DUNDEE

The event involving the hospitals occurred in the 1590s when James VI made two grants to the Templars of St Anthony. The first, in 1590, was for an operative hospital; the second, in around 1593, was for a chapel, monastery and another hospital at Leith.[25] The hospital at Leith was later founded in 1614 and called the King James Hospital.

On 27 July 1689, Bonnie Dundee was killed leading his men to victory against Crown forces at the Battle of Killiecrankie; specifically, he was hit in the left side of his ribcage by a stray musket ball. His tunic is said to have borne the Templars' Grand (eight-pointed platte) Cross.[26] If this is correct, there is strong evidence that the Templars had continued to independently exist among the Scottish highlanders for the past 100 years.

Bonnie Dundee's death had a devastating impact on the Jacobites. A succinct description is found in *Scotland: the Story of a Nation*, where the author makes the observation that:

> The loss of their leader was a crushing blow for the Jacobites. Dundee, and only Dundee, could weld the untamed clansmen into an army; it was his personality and dash which had held it together. His death destroyed any hope of Jacobite success.[27]

To understand what happened at Killiecrankie, an extended discussion is necessary. Killiecrankie is a narrow pass on the main road between Perth in the lowlands, and Inverness in the highlands. The battle occurred after Parliament had declared that James II had abdicated his throne. On 13 February 1689 William III and Mary II were proclaimed joint monarchs of Britain. This was accepted without dispute in England, but in parts of Scotland a division arose between the 'Williamites' and the 'Jacobites'. On 14 March 1689 a convention of Scottish Estates was held to determine who would rule Scotland. Both William III and James II sent letters to the convention. The letter from James was rambling and vague, and the convention vote went overwhelmingly to William III and Mary II. But the result was not taken well in some areas of the Scottish highlands.[28]

To quell any uprising in the north, the Duke of Hamilton arranged for William III to send about 4,000 to 5,000 troops to Scotland under the command of Major General Hugh Mackay. But this did not go unnoticed. In response, Bonnie Dundee raised a force of between 2,000 and 2,500 highlanders. They met in the Killiecrankie gorge. Unfortunately for the Williamites, they were at the bottom of the gorge. The Jacobites were above on the high ground. On the evening of 27 July 1689, with the setting sun at their backs, Dundee's troops charged. The Williamites were overwhelmed and ran. Very few escaped. However, the Jacobites may have won the battle at Killiecrankie, but they lost the war. Not only did they lose Viscount Dundee, they lost from a third to a half of their troops. The next battle of Dunkeld was a standoff, and effectively ended the Jacobite movement until 1745.

The authors of *The Temple and the Lodge* argue very persuasively that when Bonnie Dundee fell at Killiecrankie he was Grand Master of the Templars in Scotland, and wore the eight-pointed Grand Cross of the Order on his tunic. But the point is disputed by the author of *The Rosslyn Hoax?* who disputes the sources cited in *The Temple and the Lodge*.[29] But the authors of *The Temple and the Lodge*, *The Rosslyn Hoax?* and even the authors of 'The *Beauceant* records of the Chivalric & Military Order of the Temple of Jerusalem, Scotland', are all arguing a point of view and have a point to make. The authors of the sources cited in *The Temple and the Lodge* do not. We will never know if Bonnie Dundee was in fact a Templar, but it appears that he was. And if he was, it follows that he was joined by many other highlanders, and the Order continued to exist.

BONNIE PRINCE CHARLIE

After the death of Viscount Dundee, it is generally accepted that John Erskine, Earl of Mar, followed Viscount Dundee as the Scottish Grand Master. Upon John Erskine's death, he was succeeded by the Duke of Atholl who assumed the administrative duties of the Order as regent. Then, in 1745 at the Palace of Holyrood, Prince Charles Edward Stuart was elected Grand Master of the Knights Templar. According to *Statutes of the Religious and Military Order of The Temple*, his confirmation is affirmed in a letter dated 30 September 1745 from the Duke of Perth to Lord Ogilvy, eldest son of the Earl of Airlie. The significant portion of this letter states:

> It is truly a proud thing to see our Prince [Charles Edward Stuart] in the Palace of his fathers, with all the best blood of Scotland around him; he is much beloved of all sorts, and we cannot fail to make that pestilent England smoke for it. Upon Monday last, there was a great ball at the palace, and on Tuesday, [24 September] by appointment, there was a solemn chapter of the ancient chivalry of the temple of Jerusalem, held in the audience room; not more than ten Knights were present, for since my

lord of mar demitted the office of G. master, no general meeting has been called, save in your own north convent: Our noble Prince looked most gallantly in the white robe of the order, took his profession like a worth Knight, and after receiving congratulations of all present, did vow that he would restore the Temple higher than it was in the days of William the Lyon: then my Lord of Athol did demit as Regent, and his Royal Highness was elected G. master. I write you this knowing how you love the Order.[30]

Prince Charles's celebration at Holyrood was his last. He and his armies won several of the early battles, and there are many who believe that had he not been ill-advised as to the strength and position of the Crown troops, he would have become King of England and Scotland. But this was not the result. The result occurred at the Battle of Culloden where he was soundly defeated. He ultimately fled to Rome where he died.

The defeat of Prince Charles and the Jacobites at Culloden prevented the Templars from remaining public and visible. They had to become a secret Order that could not practice its ceremonies in public for fear of prosecution. But they did continue to exist. Some linked up with the Masonic Templars in England and Ireland. Some of the Templars simply went underground. But the Scottish Knights Templar did continue. Prince Charles was their Grand Master until his death in Rome in 1788, and he was followed by John Oliphant, Esquire of Bachilton, who died in 1795. After his death, there was no election.

ALEXANDER DEUCHAR AND THE REBIRTH OF THE TEMPLARS

The Templars in Scotland that continued were few, difficult to trace, and disorganized. The lack of a Templar leader may have been due to the attitude of the government, or to a command from Cardinal de York, the last of the direct Stewart line. But whatever the reason, the Templars continued in a state of anarchy, and did not surface until after Cardinal de York's death in 1807. Then, Alexander Deuchar, a seal engraver in Edinburgh, was elected Commander of the Edinburgh Templars.[31] This begins a saga.

Alexander Deuchar's first acts were to annul the efforts that had been made to form a union with Masonic Templary, to declare the

independence of the Templars, and to renew the Templars' ancient pre-
rogative. His goal, many say his vision, was to unite the various Templar
factions that had come into existence in Scotland, England, Ireland and
Europe. But, because the Templars in these separate geographical areas
had conflicting goals, his efforts were ultimately unsuccessful. But his
achievements were many, significant and lasting.

In 1810 Alexander Deuchar organized and commenced a Grand
Conclave of Knights Templar in Scotland. Not only was he appointed
Grand Master for life, his initial orders were confirmed. The representatives unanimously resolved to rest their claims on the general belief
of the well-accredited tradition handed down from their forefathers.[32]
The Conclave also agreed to have Prince Edward, Duke of Kent, a
chevalier du temple, become the patron protector of the Order in
north Britain. For the next two and a half decades, Alexander Deuchar,
with the help of his brother David, selflessly attempted to unite the
Templars. Deuchar was so committed to his goal of unification that in
1832 he offered to relinquish his office of Grand Master to Sir Walter
Scott, who declined for health reasons.

On 7 December 1825 Alexander Deuchar successfully proposed that
the Templars wear a long white mantle with a red eight-pointed cross that
was placed over the left breast. This tradition has continued, and today
the red eight-pointed cross is worn by many of the Scottish Templars. By
1827, Alexander Deuchar was meeting with some success in his efforts
for unification. The French Knights and others on the continent were
being incorporated into the Scottish Grand Conclave. But on the west
coast a Scott-Irish faction of the Templars, led by its own Grand Master
Sir Robert Martin, rebelled and created a schism. This group claimed
a separate, direct line of Templars from 1147 that had not been extin-
guished in 1307 or 1312. Their main claim was that the Duke of Kent was
a Hanoverian, and did not have any authority to be the Order's patron.
This caused Deuchar to seek a new patron. The primary candidate was
the Duke of Sussex, Earl of Inverness, who was a Templar, and the Grand
Prior of the French Templars in Britain. But he declined, and the problem remained unresolved until 1836. This also brought to light an issue
that had been smoldering for some time: whether a Templar need also
be a Mason.[33] The issue was never completely resolved, and as a result, in
line with the tradition beginning in 1147, the wholly independent *Militi
Templi Scotia*, or Scottish Knights Templar, came into being.

Alexander Deuchar served as Grand Master until 1836, when he was indelicately removed from the office he was elected to hold for life, in the organization he had formed. The process began in 1830 when the group of dissidents attempted to remove Deuchar as Grand Master. This effort was unsuccessful and Deuchar continued. But he secretly signed a resignation in 1831 and entrusted it to Sir Patrick Walker, another knight. On 12 January 1836 Deuchar was able to reunite the dissidents who had sought to depose him. Ironically, on that same day, Sir Patrick tendered Deuchar's 1831 resignation which was accepted. Admiral Sir David Milne, G.C.B. was then elected Grand Master. After 1836 Deuchar had nothing to do with the overall Knights Templar organization. But he continued as a member of the *Militi Templi Scotia* until he died in 1844.

The Knights Templar continued to exist, but nothing further was heard about the Knights Templar in Scotland until the middle of the twentieth century.[34] But as described in the next chapter, the Scottish Knights Templar continued to actively exist separately, and apart from the Masons. Thanks to Alexander Deuchar, the Templars in Scotland had formed numerous alliances with their brethren in Europe, especially in the Netherlands, Luxembourg and France. These alliances also continued.

NOTES

1 *Statutes of the Religious and Military Order of The Temple, as Established in Scotland with An Historical Notice of the Order,* 'Historical Notice of the Order' printed by authority of the Grand Conclave, 1843, 2nd edn, Alex, Laurie and Co. (Edinburgh, 1964), p. v. It has been argued that the 'Historical Notice', which acts as an introduction to the *Statutes,* was authored by W.I. Aytoun, Professor of Rhetoric ad Belles Lettres at Edinbugh University. See: Baigent, Michael and Leigh, Richard, *The Temple and the Lodge,* Arcade Publishing (New York, 1989), p. 280, Note 7. Others who may have been involved were J. Linning Woodman, who is said to have been the Grand Secretary and Registrar of the Order, 1842–1854, Walter Arnott, and Murray Pringle.

2 Gardner, Lawrence, *Bloodline of the Holy Grail,* Barnes & Noble (New York, 1997), p. 272.

3 *Statutes,* p. viii.

4 Ibid., pp. xiii–xiv.

5 Ibid., p. xiv.

6 Cowan, Ian B., Mackay, P.H.R. & Macquarrie, Alan, *The Knights of St. John of Jerusalem in Scotland*, Scottish Historical Society, Clark Constable Ltd (Edinburgh, 1983), p. xxx.

7 Cowan, *et al.*, *Knights of St. John of Jerusalem In Scotland*, p. 158.

8 Ralls, Karen, *Knights Templar Encyclopedia*, New Page Books (Franklin Lakes, 2007), pp. 189–190.

9 Cowan, *et al.*, *The Knights of St. John of Jerusalem In Scotland*, p. lxviii.

10 Ibid., p. lxviii.

11 Scott, Ronald McNair, *Robert the Bruce, King of Scots*, Carroll & Graf Publishers (New York, 1996), p. 228.

12 The Turcopolier was third in the Templar military hierarchy. He commanded the light cavalry and the sergeant brothers. He normally led the charges.

13 Barbour, John, *The Brus*, compiled 1375, translated by George Eyre-Todd, Gowans & Gray Limited (Glasgow, 1907), p. 228.

14 Sinclair, Andrew, *The Sword and the Grail*, Birlinn Limited (Edinburgh, 2002), p. 5.

15 Cowan, *et al.*, *The Knights of St. John of Jerusalem In Scotland*, pp. xxxviii–xl, 162. Coutts, Rev. Alfred, *The Knights Templar in Scotland*, (Edinburgh, 1890), p. 13.

16 J. Maidment, *Temparia* (Edinburgh, 1828–30), cited in Ralls, *The Templars and the Grail*, p. 114. Also, see Ralls, *Knights Templar Encyclopedia*, p. 190. The original document is quoted in Burnes, James, *Sketch of the History of the Knights Templar*, Wm. Blackwood & Sons (Edinburgh, 1840), p. xlvii.

17 Baigent and Leigh, *The Temple and the Lodge*, p. 99.

18 National Archives of Scotland, Document No. GD119/34.

19 Ibid., Document No. GD119/35.

20 Baigent and Leigh, *The Temple and the Lodge*, p. 99, citing Seton, *A History of the Family of Seton*, vol. ii, p. 751.

21 Michael, HRH Prince of Albany, *The Forgotten Monarchy of Scotland*, Element (Shaftesbury, Dorset, 1998), pp. 116–117.

22 *Statutes*, p. xv.

23 Ibid., p. xv; Baigent and Leigh, *The Temple and the Lodge*, p. 99.

24 Jacobites were members of the political movement dedicated to the restoration of the Stuarts to the British throne. The name is derived from the Latin form of James, *Jacobus*. The connection with the Templars is claimed to be

supported by the histories of the *Militi Templi Scotia* and the Scottish Grand Priory in Scotland.

25 Michael, HRH, *The Forgotten Monarchy of Scotland*, p. 117, citing 'The Privy Seal Register of Scotland'.

26 Baigent and Leigh, *The Temple and the Lodge*, pp. 165–166. Standing, Howard, *The Scottish Knights Templar, Outremer*, privately published (10 April 1995), p. 11. Michael, HRH, *The Forgotten Monarchy of Scotland*, p. 151 describes it as the Grand Cross and Sash of the Templars, and cites 'The *Beauceant* records of the Chivalric & Military Order of the Temple of Jerusalem, Scotland'.

27 Magnusson, Magnus, *Scotland: the Story of a Nation*, Atlantic Monthly Press (New York, 2000), pp. 516–518.

28 The reasons for James II's loss of the Crown are beyond the scope of this book. They are summarized by Magnus Magnusson in *Scotland: the Story of a Nation*, pp. 510–514.

29 Cooper, Robert L.D., *The Rosslyn Hoax? Viewing Rosslyn Chapel from a new perspective*, Lewis (UK, 2006), p. 79.

30 *Statutes*, pp. xvi–xvii.

31 Alexander Deuchar was first located in the High Street area and later at various addresses in the New Town. From 1832 he was designated 'seal engraver to His Majesty and genealogical agent'. National Archives of Scotland, Document No. GD1/1020.

32 Burnes, *Sketch of the History of the Knights Templar*, Wm. Blackwood & Sons (Edinburgh, 1840), pp. 72–73.

33 The relationship between the Masons and the Templars is beyond the scope of this book. The reader is referred to Magnusson & Lomas.

34 A review of the Edinburgh newspapers' archives from 1871 reveals nothing other than the attendance of Templars, or guests in Templar garb, at various balls and social gatherings.

11

THE MODERN SCOTTISH KNIGHTS TEMPLAR

One cannot discuss the Templars in Scotland without knowing about the general Templar organization. Today, the subject does not involve the basics such as lifestyle and warfare that were applicable in the thirteenth and fourteenth centuries. Today, unfortunately, much of the focus of the major Templar Orders seems to be on politics and empire building. The primary sites of the current Templar Orders are in Europe and the United States. But the political gambits of the European and United States Templars do not affect the internal workings of the Scottish Templar Orders. They do have an impact on their relationships and history, however. Because these relationships are mentioned in the discussions of the various Scottish Templar Orders, the events that lead up to the current situation are discussed first, followed by a description of the current Scottish Templar Orders.

THE ORDO SUPREMUS MILITARIS TEMPLI HIEROSOLYMITANI[1]

There are now two *Ordo Supremus Militaris Templi Hierosolymitani* (OSMTH). One is currently headquartered in Portugal; the location of the other changes every three to six years with the election of a new grand commander, the office of Grand Master now being ceremonial. These two separate Orders exist because in 1995–96 there was a schism within the OSMTH. Just as there are two points of view regarding the

Templars' continuation, there are now at least two organizations that claim to be the true continuation of the original Order that existed after the death of Jacques de Molay. This controversy originated with a coup within the OSMTH. To understand why this situation exists, it is necessary to briefly discuss the history in the OSMTH.

Prior to his death, Jacques de Molay is believed to have transferred the office of Grand Master to his Seneschal Johannes Marcus Larmenius. Around 1324, Larmenius transferred the office to Franciscus Theobaklus through a document known as the Charter of Transmission, or the Charter of Larmenius. This charter, with the approval of the Grand Council, transmitted the office of Grand Master to the next ranking Templar. After 1324, the practices set forth in the charter were generally followed by the international Templar Order until 1960 with the death of the then regent. Then, in the 1990s, a major schism occurred.

The events that led to the schism began after 1935, when Emile Clement Joseph Isaac Vandenberg, KGC of Belgium, was the prince regent and guardian of the Order.[2] As guardian, he was custodian of the Templars' records and historical documents. Because of the Second World War, and the threat of Adolf Hitler, he moved the Templar offices and archives to the safety of Portugal. Unwittingly, he placed them in the possession of Antonio Campbell Pinto de Sousa Fontes, GC. At the end of the war, Count de Sousa Fontes refused to return the records and documents to the prince regent in Belgium. Prince Regent Vandenberg passed away and there was no one to effectively challenge the count. As a result, Count de Sousa Fontes became regent of the OSMTH by magisterial decree.

In 1960 Count de Sousa Fontes died. In violation of the Charter of Larmenius, but in compliance with Portuguese law, he willed the regency to his son, Fernando Campello Pinto Pereiro de Sousa Fontes, rather than to the next ranking Templar. The problem was compounded by the fact that while the father had aggressively expanded the Knights Templar, the actions of the son did not demonstrate the qualities of leadership necessary for one who is vested with the office of regent or Grand Master. He did not pay enough attention to the growing Templar movement, either in Scotland or in the United States.

A conflict between the Templars in the United States and Count de Sousa Fontes the younger then developed. It came to a head in 1995 at a series of OSMTH conclaves in Europe led by the Sovereign Military

Order of the Temple of Jerusalem, Inc., the Templar Priory in the United States (SMOTJ, Inc.). At a series of conclaves the SMOTJ, Inc. was joined by a number of European priories and commanderies that voted to no longer recognize Count de Sousa Fontes as its regent or Grand Master. The OSMTH found that the count had violated numerous provisions of the original Templar Rule. It then revoked its allegiance to Count de Sousa Fontes and, in essence, gave him the boot.[3] The SMOTJ, Inc. then prevented Count de Sousa Fontes from having any involvement in the United States by a federal court civil lawsuit claiming trademark infringement.[4] The new OSMTH leadership now claims to be the successor to the Templar line that can be traced back to Jacques de Molay.

The situation was and is not without controversy, and has been labeled a schismatic coup led by the SMOTJ, Inc. in the United States, and dissidents in Britain, Germany and other European countries.[5] But Count de Sousa Fontes continues to lead numerous successful priories in countries throughout the world.

History may favor Count de Sousa Fontes, but results and achievements speak well for the OSMTH leadership that expelled him. The OSMTH now exists in over twenty countries through grand priories, priories, commanderies or preceptories. It has not only been recognized by the United Nations, but it has been granted special consultative status. It performs a substantial amount of humanitarian and charitable work, not only in Israel and the Palestinian Territories, but around the world. But Count de Sousa Fontes was Grand Master long before 1996. As a result, there are now at least two Templar organizations with credible claims to the office of Grand Master.[6]

Today, there are numerous Templar Orders in Scotland. Some are long established. Others seem to form and dissolve quickly. Two that existed in 2006 do not appear to exist today. Some are visible, others remain in the background. Some are politically aggressive, others are passive and quietly do good works and help others. Some have cried out for recognition, others let their deeds speak for themselves.

The following should be looked at as a snapshot. Because much of it is based on oral history, it may differ from the readers' perspective. Included in the snapshot are the Grand Priory of Scotland; the *Militi Templi Scotia*; the Autonomous Grand Priory of Scotland; Scottish Knight Templars; the Grand Priory of the Knights Templar in Scotland; The Rosslyn Templars; and Grand Priory of the Scots.

The history of the Templars, and in particular those in Scotland, is not unlike that of its clans; it is rife with conflict and controversy. Each seeks the same goals, yet each tends to characterize its identity as unique and preeminent. First, there is the dispute that applies to all Templar organizations throughout the world; that is, can today's organizations be traced back to the original Templars? There are two points of view. One argues for the continued existence of the Templars, and traces the line of Grand Masters back to Jacques de Molay.[7] The other is consistent with Pope Clement V's papal bull *Vox in excelso* of 22 March 1312, that abolished the existence of the Order by 'inviolable and perpetual decree'.[8] There is also the question of whether the Order traces its origin back to Jacques de Molay and his successor Johannes Marcus Larmenius to the *Ordo Supremus Militaris Templi Hierosolymitani*, or back through Scotland to the Templars that existed there during the Scottish Templar inquisition and the Battle of Bannockburn. Also, the origin of several of the Orders is complicated by the coup within the OSMTH, and the fact that there are now two such organizations with two Grand Masters: the original organization headed by Count de Sousa Fontes in Portugal, and the new leadership that is currently headed by Rear Admiral James J. Carey. The questions have a significant importance in Scotland because of the minimal, direct evidence of a continued Templar presence in Scotland after 1314.

THE GRAND PRIORY OF SCOTLAND

In April 1961 his Excellency Baron Anton Leuprecht was Mondial Chief (coordinator) of all Autonomous Grand Priories throughout the world on behalf of Count de Sousa Fontes. His jurisdiction included Scotland, and ultimately Canada and the United States. In 1962 Baron Leuprecht began the creation of a new Grand Priory of Scotland. The Scottish Grand Priory became active in January 1972 with the appointment of Francis Andrew Sherry, Knight Grand Cross of the Temple, as Grand Prior of the Grand Priorate of Scotland. This appointment was confirmed by Baron Leuprecht.[9]

The newly formed Grand Priory of Scotland was and is autonomous. Its affiliation as an Associate of the OSMTH under Count de Sousa Fontes was reaffirmed in 1978 by Baron Leuprecht, when he formally stated that the Charter of the Grand Priory of Scotland was autonomous.[10] After the schism in 1995–96, it became an Associated Autonomous Priory with the new OSMTH. But it later found that it could not comply with the demands of the new leadership of the OSMTH, and then continued as an autonomous priory.

For a time, the Order was an active and visible Scottish priory. After 1972 the Grand Priory of Scotland undertook a significant amount of charitable work. It contributed to the work of the Highland and Island Eventide Homes for Elderly Sects, and to the setting up of a Gaelic library in Skye at the Gaelic College (Sabbal Mor Ostaig). Steps were also taken to protect buildings and places of historic and architectural importance to Scotland. Whenever possible these buildings were used for Templar ceremonies. This was in line with its original published objectives, which were: to carry out works of welfare and charity and to protect the national culture of Scotland; to perpetuate the chivalric traditions of knighthood; to be a patron of historical, heraldic and genealogical studies concerning the Order and all Orders of knighthood connected with the Order; and to support the preservation and restoration of historic buildings and places.[11]

One of the activities that made the Grand Priory of Scotland well known was the Soirée of the White Cockade. This was an annual formal ball that was held to celebrate Prince Charles Edward Stuart's audience for the Templars on 24 September 1745 at the Palace of Holyrood.[12] There were many memorable soirées, but two stand out. The first was the Soirée in 1979 that was attended by HRH Prince Michael James Stewart of Albany, the claimed heir of Prince Charles Edward Stuart.[13] Because of his friendship with the Grand Prior Francis Sherry, HRH Prince Michael James Stewart of Albany was invested into the Grand Priory of Scotland. His first public appearance as a Templar was at the Soirée that same year. The next significant soirée occurred in 1985 when it was attended by Count de Sousa Fontes, his wife the Contess de Sousa Fontes, together with a number of their friends who were also members of Portuguese nobility.[14] The Soirées of the White Cockade began in 1974 and continued until 1985.

By 1986 the expanding Grand Priory of Scotland had bailiwicks in the east of Scotland, the Borders, Strathclyde, and the west of Scotland. It had commanderies in Stirling, central Scotland and in Edinburgh. It had additional preceptories at Inchinnan, Glasgow, Edinburgh,

Galloway and Jedburgh, with future developments at Falkirk, Inverness and Aberdeen. Efforts were also begun to establish a unit in North America which would be linked to the Order in Scotland. This resulted in the formation of what became the Bailiwick of Nova Scotia.[15]

But the Grand Priory of Scotland was often involved in controversy. The details are beyond the purpose of this book, but their nature can be inferred from the events. In December 1989 the Grand Priory of Scotland was considered to be apostate by the Grand Magistral Council in Portugal. Although under suspension, the Grand Priory of Scotland considered itself to be autonomous and continued to function. Then in late 1992 and early 1993 the Grand Priory of Scotland split into a number of different Orders. Three survive today. The largest group of knights formed the *Militi Templi Scotia*. Another, led by James McGrath, formed what became known as the Scottish Knight Templars, and the third is the Chivalric Military Order of the Temple of Jerusalem, led by its Grand Prior Kevin Shirra. The first two have been the most visible, have gone through some changes, and will be discussed in some detail. The Chivalric Military Order of the Temple of Jerusalem is one of those Orders that quietly does good works and helps others.

THE MILITI TEMPLI SCOTIA (1993–2009)

The *Militi Templi Scotia* was formed in 1993 by a large group of knights from the Grand Priory of Scotland. Its aims are to serve God and Scotland through its activities, which are: to help preserve, and be the guardians of Scotland's traditions, culture and heritage; to promote chivalry, and promulgate the understanding of Scotland's history; and to support charitable interests.

The organization's primary goal is to provide an opportunity to serve. As it evolved, it claimed to trace its origins to the reformation of the Templar Order in Scotland in 1789 under Alexander Deuchar.[16] A fascinating aspect of the *Militi Templi Scotia* is the fact that it claimed to be the custodian of what is possibly the original Stone of Scone.

The Stone of Scone, sometimes called the Stone of Destiny or the Stone of Dunnad, was brought to Scotland from Ireland by Fergus

Mor mac Eirc (Fergus I) in around 485, when he and his brothers conquered the areas in the south-west of Scotland, and he became the
first king of Dál Riata in Argyll.[17] Fergus Mor mac Eirc was crowned
while sitting on the Stone at Dunnad, as were each of the subsequent
kings and queens of Scotland, until 8 August 1296 when a stone, believed
to be the Stone of Scone, was taken from Scone to Westminster Abbey
in London by King Edward I. It remained there until very early on
Christmas Day in 1950 when four students removed it from under the
royal throne at Westminster Abbey. The stone was then returned in April
1953. It was formally returned to Scotland on 30 November 1996. But
is this the true Stone of Scone? The Stone that was taken to London by
King Edward I was described as:

> A quarry dressed block of coarse grained old red sandstone, measuring
> 26 ½ inches by 16 ½ inches by 11 inches thick. On it is a roughly incised
> cross, and an oblong indentation. It is fitted at the ends with iron sta-
> ples, carrying rings which are so attached that a pole can easily be passed
> through them to facilitate carrying it. These cuttings are probably of the
> time of Edward.[18]

In fact, the *Militi Templi Scotia* contended that the actual Stone of Scone
was not the one taken to England by Edward I in 1296, and that it has
never left Scotland. Is this true? Is the Stone of Scone taken by King
Edward I Scotland's coronation stone? Or before King Edward I could
get to Scone, was the stone switched? The *Militi Templi Scotia* would have
told you that it had been switched, and that it had the original. The
records of the Royal Commission on Historical Monuments indicate
that today's Stone of Scone, now at Stirling Castle, is the original. But
many Scots dispute both of these claims.

The *Militi Templi Scotia* was independent. As described later in this
chapter, in March 2005 the OSMTH asked the *Militi Templi Scotia's*
representatives to join a consortium for joint recognition. Its representatives listened quietly, and said the proposal would be considered. The
Militi Templi Scotia remained independent. But in May 2006, a number
of its members left and formed The Commandery of Jacques de Molay
1314. The remainder continued as the *Militi Templi Scotia*, but became
relatively inactive.

THE AUTONOMOUS GRAND PRIORY OF SCOTLAND

The Autonomous Grand Priory of Scotland is the surviving priory after a controversy within the *Militi Templi Scotia* that occurred in 2006. The result of the controversy was that part of the *Militi Templi Scotia*, its Commandery of Jacques de Molay 1314, formally separated from the *Militi Templi Scotia*. It then formed a new and separate organization with that name at Rosslyn Chapel. Its raison d'être was and is: to endeavor to promote Scotland's history and preserve its culture, traditions and heritage; to seek the truth in the study and development of Templarism; to pursue chivalric Christian ideals and to support charitable causes; and to host and to act as pathfinders for international Templars and pilgrims visiting Scotland.

The Commandery of Jacques de Molay 1314 was so successful that it resulted in the formation of a new grand priory, the Autonomous Grand Priory of Scotland. This occurred at a ceremony in the chapel at Balgonie Castle on 9 May 2009. Several of its members stand out. Robert Brydon is an honorary member who owns numerous Templar artifacts and materials. When he was a member of the original Grand Priory of Scotland, he formed a group known as *Stella Templum* to study them. A number of his artifacts have been displayed at Rosslyn Chapel. Bill Hunter is a direct descendent of the family of Alexander Deuchar and is the family historian.

The Autonomous Grand Priory of Scotland does not purport to possess the Stone of Scone. Its Grand Prior is George Stewart who was the original commander of the Commandery of Jacques de Molay 1314. He will hold the position of Grand Prior for five years. The Autonomous Grand Priory of Scotland is affiliated with neither Count de Sousa Fontes nor the new OSMTH. The OSMTH's and de Sousa Fontes' Orders require that each Order and its members have no contact or recognition of the other. The Autonomous Grand Priory of Scotland recognizes all invested Templars whether they are affiliated with the OSMTH or Count de Sousa Fontes.

As with the *Militi Templi Scotia* and other Templar Orders, it is open only to Christians. Membership is not available upon application, but by invitation. Details of the Autonomous Grand Priory of Scotland can be found at its website.[19]

THE SCOTTISH KNIGHT TEMPLARS/GRAND PRIORY OF SCOTLAND

When James McGrath left the Grand Priory of Scotland, he ultimately founded and became the grand prior of an Order variously known as The Scottish Knight Templars or the Sovereign Scottish Knights of Christ, Temple of Jerusalem, as well as several other names. The Order is autonomous, independent and non-Masonic. Under James McGrath, the Scottish Knight Templars claimed to trace its lineage back to Hughes de Payens through Charles Edward Stuart and Viscount Dundee, James Graham of Claverhouse (Bonnie Dundee). Like most of the other Scottish priories, the Scottish Knight Templars traces its modern origin from Baron Anton Leuprecht and Francis Andrew Sherry. But it appears to be the only one that continued to be 'associated' with and recognized by the original OSMTH under Grand Master Count de Sousa Fontes.

There seems to exist a degree of rancor between the Order and the others that originated from the efforts of Baron Anton Leuprecht, because the Order, under the name Grand Priory of Scotland, claims that in October 1989 it divested Francis Andrew Sherry of all ranks, offices and titles. This is rather inconsistent with events, however, because in May 1991, Francis Sherry, as grand prior of the Grand Priory of Scotland, invested seventy knights and dames into the Order at Ontario, California, USA.

James McGrath's control of the Order was ardent and strident. The Order would have absolutely nothing to do with those who did not recognize Count de Sousa Fontes or had anything to do with Masonry. It ended in 2007 when he resigned as grand prior and was expelled from the Order. The Order then became the Grand Priory of Scotland. James McGrath was replaced by Gordon McGregor Comrie, who was installed as grand prior at a ceremony at Balantrodoch Temple. On 17 March 2008 the Grand Priory of Scotland's association with Count de Sousa Fontes came full circle and the Order was re-charted into his OSMTH (Regency). Finally, in September 2008 the Order's Grand Master decreed that James McGrath was formally divested of all ranks, offices and privileges of the Order and he was suspended for life.[20] With the expulsion of James McGrath from the Order, and his expulsion from the Templars, the website for the Scottish Knights Templar was taken down.

The Grand Priory of Scotland now has priories of North America and Australia, and a NATO Bailiwick of Italy. Its aims and objectives have been expanded towards fostering mediation and universal tolerance. Candidates are welcome to membership so long as they are practicing Christians. Membership is by application and, upon initial acceptance, the applicant must serve a six-month candidacy before he or she can become a knight.

THE GRAND PRIORY OF THE KNIGHTS TEMPLAR IN SCOTLAND

The new OSMTH administration recognizes only one Templar organization in each country. In 2005 there were at least three autonomous Templar priories in Scotland. Two of them, the Scottish Knights Templar and the *Militi Templi Scotia*, had an alliance or some relationship with the OSMTH. In March 2005 the OSMTH held a conference near Edinburgh with the goal of resolving the issue of having recognition for only one Scottish entity. Its solution was that the Orders in Scotland form some sort of an alliance or consortium among themselves and appoint one person as their joint representative. All of the representatives remained very courteous.[21] But each heralded its autonomy. In terms of selecting a joint representative, each group's representatives left the conference saying they would look into it. But Scots being Scots, none could agree to be part of another organization in which a member of another Order would have access to the international Order. As a result, each of the organizations remain autonomous.

The OSMTH's solution appears to have been the formation of a new grand priory in Scotland, the Grand Priory of the Knights Templar in Scotland, through colonization by the Grand Priory of France. The addition of another priory in Scotland seems a bit redundant. The new Order is now fully recognized by the new OSMTH, but it does not appear to have anything approaching the success of the other Scottish priories.

The Grand Priory of the Knights Templar in Scotland is also a charitable organization. It works with the United Nations Association UK in areas which stress education and youth programs, and the Glasgow Homeless Partnership in conjunction with the Silent Knight, an anonymous charity and mentoring programme.[22]

THE ROSSLYN TEMPLARS

The Rosslyn Templars is an organization which is primarily visible through its website.[23] It is dedicated to researching Freemasonry, Rosslyn Chapel and the Knights Templar. It is devoted to the promotion and interpretation of Rosslyn Chapel from a number of different disciplines. While its name includes reference to the Knights Templar, it focuses to a great extent on the Templar aspects of Freemasonry. At the current time it is an information source only, and does not communicate with those visiting the website.

It is also a non-profit organization, and accepts contributions for charity, favoring the Children's Hospice Association for Scotland.

THE GRAND PRIORY OF THE SCOTS

The largest Scottish Templar organization had its beginnings in Scotland, existed in Nova Scotia, is now led by HE Raymond Morris of Balgonie and Eddergoll and functions in the United States.

The Grand Priory of the Scots began as the 'Scottish Templars in North America' in Nova Scotia in the late 1980s. The Commandery of Nova Scotia was formed for specifically the benefit of Scots living outside Scotland and was affiliated with the Grand Priory of Scotland. In an attempt to retain control in Scotland, its investitures were initially held in Scotland. In 1989 the first investiture of North American knights was held at St Mary's Episcopal Cathedral in Edinburgh. In 1990 nineteen North Americans were invested in Scotland at Rosslyn Chapel. In the meantime, the Commandery of Nova Scotia was elevated to the designation of a bailiwick.[24] In April 1991 Grand Master Count de Sousa Fontes formally elevated the Bailiwick of Nova Scotia to the status of an independent, non-territorial grand priory. In order to prevent any possible confusion in North America, the name of the grand priory was changed to The Grand Priory of the Scots. This priory then became active in the United States. The membership there grew, and then separated from the members in Nova Scotia. The majority of the knights living in Nova Scotia then formed a new commandery that joined the SMOTJ, Inc.

The citizens of the United States are independent, and it wasn't long before the Grand Priory of the Scots in the United States became independent. The requirement for investitures in Scotland ended after December 1990, when the Nova Scotia Priory of Robert the Bruce planned its investiture in the United States – specifically in Ontario, California. The fact that the investiture was planned for Ontario, California, instead of Ontario, Canada was not by coincidence. The investiture was intended for a very large number of new knights who lived in the United States. It was designed to demonstrate that there were a substantial number of people in the United States who were linked to Scotland, but who were separate from those in Nova Scotia. The investiture took place in May 1991. The grand prior of the Grand Priory of Scotland conducted the investiture and invested more than seventy knights and dames.[25]

In June 1991 Grand Master Count de Sousa Fontes confirmed that the USA was a grand priory that existed independently of the Grand Priory of Scotland. HE Raymond Morris of Balgonie and Eddergoll became the Grand Prior elect of the Grand Priory of the Scots in the United States. His position was confirmed and he holds it today.

On 25 June 1998, allegedly as a result of the judgment in SMOTJ, Inc. *v.* de Sousa Fontes, the Grand Priory of the Scots was required to join and become affiliated with the SMOTJ, Inc. through a fully executed written contract that was drafted by the attorneys for the SMOTJ, Inc. But then, on 28 December 2007, it repudiated its own written contract. Seventeen Templars had transferred from the Grand Priory of the Scots to the SMOTJ, Inc. When the Grand Priory of the Scots dropped them from its roles, the SMOTJ, Inc. accused the Grand Priory of the Scots of denying its members dual membership, of being 'un-Christian, and not in the true spirit of Templarism'. These claims border on the absurd. The Grand Priory of the Scots did not deny that its prior members continued to be Templars. In addition, the comments of SMOTJ, Inc. disregard practicality, common sense, and historical tradition which is demonstrated by the movement of Walter de Clifton in the late thirteenth and early fourteenth centuries from the houses in Yorkshire, to London, to Wiltshire, to Lincolnshire in England, and then to Balantrodoch as the Master of Scotland. He was always a Templar, but was only involved in one Templar house at a time, not five simultaneously.

The Grand Priory of the Scots has three priories, and numerous commanderies and preceptories. It is a non-profit Order that focuses its work on those in need in the United States. Its efforts cover a broad spectrum including in kind and financial help to those in need, to direct financial assistance to numerous other charitable organizations. Membership is by invitation.

In 1307 the Templar Order was brought down largely by its arrogance. But it has survived in Scotland as well as in Europe. It is hoped that the conflict between the international Orders and the attitude of some of their members will not lead to history repeating itself. But in terms of Scotland, the Scottish priories are now very strong and will continue.

NOTES

1   The international organization uses the Latin name for the 'Sovereign Military Order of the Temple of Jerusalem'.

2   At that time there was no Grand Master.

3   Specifically, the count was expelled for theft in accordance with Templar Rule 227. Thys, Leo, *History of The Order of the Temple of Jerusalem*, Stewart Graphics, p. 68.

4   SMOTJ, Inc. *v.* de Sousa Fontes, case No. U.S.D.C. Tex. No. 3-995CV-0890G. The salient facts are:

The SMOTJ, Inc. in the United States is incorporated in the state of New Jersey as 'The Sovereign Military Order of the Temple of Jerusalem, Inc.' In 1993 the SMOTJ, Inc. registered a number of Templar insignias, and mottos (including the patriarchal cross, which was in the public domain and had been used by many long before the SMOTJ was incorporated) with the US Trademark Office. The trademarks were granted in 1995.

The SMOTJ, Inc. then filed a lawsuit in Federal Court against Fernando de Sousa Fontes. This came to an end on 12 November 1996, when the SMOTJ obtained a default judgment against not only Count de Sousa Fontes, but all persons acting in concert or participation with him. This meant that anyone involved with de Sousa Fontes was prevented from using the SMOTJ's trademarks.

5   Olsen, Oddvar, ed. *The Templar Papers*, Career Press (Franklin Lakes, 2006), p. 104.

6   There is another group that separated from Count de Sousa Fontes known as the International Federated Alliance that does not appear to currently involve itself in Scotland.

7 Burnes, James, *Sketch of the History of the Knights Templar*, Wm. Blackwood & Sons (Edinburgh, 1840), pp. 39 *et seq*. Butler, Alan and Dafoe, Stephen, *The Warriors and the Bankers, a History of the Knights Templar From 1307 to the Present*, Templar Books (Ontario, Canada, 1998).

8 Barber, Malcolm, *The New Knighthood, a History of the Order of the Temple*, Canto edition, Cambridge University Press (New York, 1994), p. 280.

9 'Templar Notes', *The Scottish Knights Templar*, published by the Stirling Commandery (January 1987), p. 16. While the Grand Priory of Scotland was recognized in 1972 by Baron Leuprecht, it was not until early 1980 that the Grand Priory of Scotland was accorded formal Limited Recognition by Count de Sousa Fontes.

10 Standing, Howard, *The Scottish Knights Templar, Outremer*, privately published (1995), p. 12.

11 'Templar Notes', *The Scottish Knights Templar*, p. 16.

12 Francis Andrew Sherry de Achaea, GCOT, Grand Prior of Scotland, 'The Templar', p. 7, undated.

13 Michael, HRH Prince of Albany, *The Forgotten Monarchy of Scotland*, Element (Shaftesbury, Dorset, 1998), p. 304. Prince Michael, also known as Michael Lefosse, claims to be a hereditary Templar, the head of the royal House of Stewart, and the rightful heir to the Scottish and English monarchy. His investiture into the Scottish Knights Templar was not without controversy. After the investiture, a number of knights and dames left the priory.

14 'Soirée of the White Cockade', *The Scottish Knight Templar* (1986–87), p. 10. National Library of Scotland.

15 Standing, *The Scottish Knights Templar, Outremer*, p. 13.

16 This was stated on the *Militi Templi Scotia*'s former website in January 2009. The author was later informed that there is a direct descendent of the Alexander Duechar family that is the family historian, and that a direct Templar line to the current Templar Orders has not been established.

17 Lane, Alan and Campbell, Ewan, *Dunadd, An Early Dalriadic Capital*, Oxbow Books (Oxford, 2000), p. 33.

18 Gerber, Pat, *Stone of Destiny*, Canongate Books Ltd (Edinburgh, 1997), p. 105, quoting the description of the Royal Commission on Historical Monuments, London.

Also, a small group of members of the Grand Priory of Scotland called Stella Templum was formed by Robert Brydon to study his Templar artifacts and body of work. Among the material is a description of four stones which are part of Scotland's heritage and culture: St Columba's seat, the Pictish Stone, the Celtic Stone, and the Stone of Destiny or the Stone of Scone. Of these, the Stone of Destiny is the most significant. It is believed that the first three stones are one and the same. Gerber, *Stone of Destiny*, p. 133.

19 www.skt.org.uk

20 The details of the Grand Priory of Scotland can be viewed at www.scot-tishtemplarknights.info.

21 This was an achievement. The author attended this conference and can truthfully say that everyone was required to sit and listen for fifteen to twenty minutes while the OSMTH's Grand Master lauded his and his organization's efforts.

22 Substantially more information can be found at the Grand Priory's website at scottishknightstemplar.org

23 www.rosslyntemplars.org.uk. It is included because a number of its references provide information about the Knights Templar that do not involve the Masons or Masonic tradition.

24 Standing, *The Scottish Knights Templar, Outremer*, p. 13.

25 HRH Michael of Albany could not attend because of travel arrangement and passport problems.

APPENDIX

COULD THERE HAVE BEEN TEMPLARS AT BANNOCKBURN?

Even with his excommunication, would the Templars have been inclined to join Robert the Bruce? If they would, would there have been enough Templars with the necessary skills to make a difference?

When considering the Templars' flight from France, the first question is, how would they have known to flee to Scotland to fight for Robert the Bruce? Much of the answer to this question is discussed in Chapter 6, 'The Templars' Flight to Scotland'. The answer to the remainder of the question can be gleaned from the information that exists from which one can create a profile of Robert the Bruce.

Robert the Bruce was born on 11 July 1274 at Turnberry Castle above the Firth of Clyde. Very little is known of his youth. In line with the custom at that time, he probably was raised by a foster mother who would educate young Robert along with her children. Young Robert would also have begun learning his fighting skills. Between his birth and 1292 there is only one written record of Robert the Bruce, a deed, which he witnessed along with his father and several others. Nothing else is known of him until he was eighteen. By then he was well educated, in excellent physical shape and well trained in fighting skills. He is described as a well-rounded, and likeable individual. Because he was in line for the Scottish throne, Bruce was raised to speak all the languages of his lineage and nation. He was fluent in Gaelic, English, of the court in London and of northern England, Norman-French, with literacy in

Latin. He could also read French. From this comes the fact that Robert the Bruce could have easily conversed with the Templars from England, and many from France.

The fighting skills of Robert the Bruce were renowned. He was ranked as one of the three most accomplished knights in Christendom, along with the Holy Roman Emperor Henry and Sir Giles D'Argentan.[1] His dispatch of John 'The Red' Comyn demonstrates Bruce's willingness to act without hesitation. Bruce's phenomenal courage was demonstrated during the first day of the Battle of Bannockburn when he met Sir Henry de Bohun, to whom King Edward I had given Bruce's lands in Annandale and Carrick, and 'brought down his axe with such force on his opponent's head that he cut through helmet, skull and brain and his axe handle shivered in two'.[2]

Formal relations between Bruce and France began in 1309 when he responded to a letter from King Philip IV, reminding him of the old alliance between the French and the Scots, and seeking assistance for a forthcoming crusade. Bruce responded cordially, and asked that his help with the crusade be postponed until 'Scotland had recovered her pristine liberty'.[3]

Robert the Bruce died on 7 June 1329 at the age of fifty-four, probably from the effects of his leprosy. His noble stature can be seen from how he is depicted by his statue at Bannockburn (see Figure 10). His experience and battles, a sword wound to the head, and a broken cheekbone among others, are etched in his face as shown on the forensic bust that was made from his skull by Dr Ian Macleod and Dr Richard Neave (see Figure 11). From the scars and creases, it is clear that Robert the Bruce was someone to be reckoned with.

From this brief profile, several conclusions can be drawn. His ranking with Holy Roman Emperor Henry in terms of fighting skills tells us that his reputation extended outside of Scotland and well into Europe. It also tells us that he would have been known to, and respected by, many of the Templar Knights. The letter of Philip IV, which was probably sent in 1308 because the response was drafted in March of 1309 at Bruce's first Parliament, works to both sides of the argument. It confirms that lines of communication existed between France and Scotland so that those in France could be aware of Bruce's excommunication. On the other hand, if France and Scotland were on friendly terms, this might have deterred some Templars from fleeing to Scotland.

Based on what happened to the Templars that were arrested, and the opportunities for freedom arising from Scotland's blanket excommunication, there is little doubt that the Templar Knights would have been eager to join Robert the Bruce.

THE TEMPLARS WHO FLED TO SCOTLAND

At the time of their arrest, the Templars existed from northern to southern Europe, and in the British Isles. It is claimed that the Templars qualified to fight at Bannockburn were killed at Acre in 1291. This is a very valid point. Recruitment continued after Acre, and the new knights had training but little front-line battle experience, and none in Outremer. And there is a significant difference between training and actual battle experience. But Robert the Bruce had thousands of troops at Bannockburn. A few tens or hundreds of additional troops would have made little difference. But were Templars available who fought in Outremer and who could have assisted Robert the Bruce as advisors?

While there is some evidence of flight from Italy and Spain to Scotland, the published statistics only cover France and England. But from this, there are several questions that can be answered. If the Knights Templar were present at Bannockburn, how old were they? Where were they from? Of what were they capable? Did they wear their white or brown tunics with the red or black cross under their left shoulder?

Those who hypothesize that the Templars were present at Bannockburn simply assume that they were there. Some assume that the Templars charged over Gillies Hill, possibly in their white tunics bearing the red Templar cross.[4] Robert L.D. Cooper assumes that they were too old to have participated at Bannockburn; that the vast majority of the Templars who could have been an effective fighting force were killed at Acre.[5] So the basic question is, at the time of their arrest in 1307, were there any Templars in France who fled and could have effectively assisted Robert the Bruce at the Battle of Bannockburn? Obviously the answer will never be known as a matter of absolute fact. But there is data available which permits approximations that are accurate enough to reach some basic conclusions.[6]

To begin, a few simple facts must be considered. Acre fell on 18 May 1291. Sixteen years later, on 13 October 1307, the French King

Philip IV sought to arrest all of the Templars. On 24 June 1314, twenty-three years after the fall of Acre, and seven years after the Templar arrests, Robert the Bruce won the Battle of Bannockburn. The median age of the new Templar recruit was his mid to late twenties. Although squires were usually knighted at the age of twenty or twenty-one, many Templars were recruited later in life. The Years of Service (YOS) of the interrogated knights supports this assumption. Further, just as today, new young recruits were quickly sent to the fighting line, which then was Outremer. And again, just like with our troops today, after a period of time in Outremer, the knights were rotated back to France, or their native country. Before the arrests, a knight generally served in the east for a period of from one and a half to three years.[7] Because the Templars lived an austere but wholesome life, if they were not killed in battle, they lived a fairly long life, into their late fifties or early sixties. In France, twenty-four per cent of the Templars who were interrogated were between the ages of fifty and fifty-nine. In addition, of those interrogated eleven per cent had lived to be between sixty and sixty-nine. A few were even older.

The age of a Templar at the time of his arrest, who could ultimately serve at Bannockburn, and who would have had service in Outremer, could have been as young as forty. Generally they would have been about forty-seven.

This age is calculated as follows:

Assumption	Years
Median age at Recruitment	27
Time of service prior to Acre	4
Time from Acre to Arrest	16
Total	47

Because 2.4 per cent of the Templars who were interrogated were under the age of twenty, the minimum age for recruitment was nineteen to twenty. Therefore, an arrested Templar who could have fought at Bannockburn was in the neighborhood of thirty-eight to thirty-nine years old for sergeants, and forty to forty-one for knights.

Assuming four YOS in Outremer, those who fought in Outremer would have had at least twenty YOS at the time of their arrest.

The range of ages of the Templar Knights who could have fought at Bannockburn would have been from forty-seven years old to approximately sixty.

This range is calculated as follows:

Assumption	Years
Earliest age of a knight at recruitment	20
Time from Acre to Bannockburn	23
Time of service prior to Acre	4
Total	47

Assuming 354 Templars were arrested in France, approximately twenty-six per cent were between the ages of forty and forty-nine, twenty-four per cent were between the ages of fifty and fifty-nine, and eleven per cent were between the ages of sixty and sixty-nine.[8] This would mean that fifty per cent of the knights in France that were not arrested would be within the age range to have fought at Bannockburn.

Also, there is the question that at the time of their arrest in 1307, were there any Templars in England who could have effectively assisted Robert the Bruce as advisors at the Battle of Bannockburn? Surprisingly, the answer seems to be some but not many. Clarence Perkins claims to have found only 144 after a careful review of the available materials.[9] Evelyn Lord reports 153 Templars were arrested in England and that a total of 170 Templars were arrested in all of England, Scotland and Ireland.[10] Of these, there were 15 knights, and 155 sergeants.[11] Twenty per cent of the Templars arrested had between twenty and thirty-three YOS, more than enough to have brought their experience to Scotland.[12]

FLIGHT TO SCOTLAND

The next question is: how many Templars actually fled to Scotland? Those who believe that the Templars did flee to Scotland speak in terms of boatloads. But this assumes that most, if not all of them, did escape to Scotland. But there is no evidence, or even estimates to support this. The best that can be done is to apply what little data there is, and make further assumptions. From the best estimates, it appears that from 210 to 355 knights avoided capture, as well as 556 to 936 sergeants, or a high of 1,291

to a low of 766 fighting men. Assume only twenty-five per cent went
to Scotland. If you assume that fifty per cent that fled had experience in
Outremer, then:

High: 355 knights/4 = 89 × 50%   44 with possible service in
                                     Outremer

        936 sergeants/4 = 234 × 50% 117 with possible service in
                                     Outremer

        Total   161

Low: 210 knights/4 = 52 × 50%   26 with possible service in
                                     Outremer

        556 sergeants/4 = 139 × 50% 69 with possible service in
                                     Outremer

        Total   95

A conservative estimate would be that fifteen per cent of those who
went to Scotland had battlefield experience in Outremer. This calculates
as follows:

High: 355 knights/4 = 89 × 15%   13 with possible service in
                                     Outremer

        936 sergeants/4 = 234 × 15% 35 with possible service in
                                     Outremer

        Total   48

Low: 210 knights/4 = 52 × 15%   8 with possible service in
                                     Outremer

        556 sergeants/4 = 139 × 15% 21 with possible service in
                                     Outremer

        Total   29

Baigent and Leigh, *The Temple and the Lodge*, discuss the Templar flight
from France as a 'mass exodus' or 'a sizable number' or 'a minimum of
1,030 active members of the military Order still at large'.[13] With this
hypothesis, there could have been notably more than from twenty-nine
to ninety-five Templars with Outremer combat experience to advise
Robert the Bruce and to have ridden with Sir Robert of Keith's cavalry.

In England, it appears that hundreds of Templars avoided arrest. In 1842 Charles G. Addison stated that 'some had escaped in disguise to the wild and mountainous parts of Wales, Scotland and Ireland'.[14] Michael Baigent and Richard Leigh argue that ninety-three military men were left at large.[15]

There is no question that the Templars in England were well aware of the coming arrests. King Edward's orders went out in December of 1307, but there were no arrests until at least 9 January 1308.[16] In addition, at first, King Edward followed English law and did not torture the arrested Templars. But later, after pressure from the Pope and King Philip IV, there was some. Thus, at first there was little reason to flee to Scotland. But this changed. And, as demonstrated by Brian de Jay, many of the Templars in England were warriors.

From the articles of Archie McKerracher and his followers that argue for the Templar presence at Bannockburn, and that of Lin Robinson in rebuttal, it is clear that the intense debate as to whether the Templars were present at Bannockburn will continue, and never be resolved. But, in answer to the question, could they actually have been at Bannockburn, the answer is clearly 'yes'. Did they wear their white or brown tunics with the red cross under their left shoulder? Considering their age, the fact that many shed their tunics when they heard of the arrests, the time between their flight and Bannockburn, and their primary function as advisors, probably not. Obviously, the final question is were they there? In coming to a conclusion, one should not forget that Robert the Bruce lived and fought in a small country where one is never more than fifty miles from a sea or ocean. Until Bannockburn, he fought small battles with only hundreds of troops. Then, in one year he successfully fought with a large, well-armed, excellently trained army that consisted of thousands of troops. Could this have happened without the help of warriors trained to fight with thousands of troops in wide and expansive theaters? Possibly. But then, possibly not!

NOTES

1 Scott, Ronald McNair, *Robert the Bruce, King of Scots*, Carroll & Graf Publishers (New York, 1996), p. 13.

2 Ibid., p. 153.

3   Barrow, G.W.S., *Robert Bruce*, University of California Press (Berkeley & Los Angeles, 1965), p. 261.

4   Sanello, Frank, *The Knights Templar, God's Warriors, the Devil's Bankers*, Taylor Trade Publishing (Lanham, 2003), p. 202; Baigent, Michael & Leigh, Richard, *The Temple and the Lodge*, Arcade Publishing (New York, 1989), p. 36; Sinclair, Andrew, *Rosslyn, The Story of Rosslyn Chapel and the True Story Behind The Da Vinci Code*, Birlinn Ltd (Edinburgh, 2006), p. 63.

5   Cooper, Robert L.D., *The Rosslyn Hoax?* Lewis (UK, 2006), p. 222.

6   Forey, Alan, 'Towards a Profile of the Templars in the Early Fourteenth Century', in Malcolm Barber, ed. *The Military Orders, Fighting for the Faith and Caring for the Sick*, Variorum, Ashgate Publishing Ltd (Aldershot, 1994), pp. 196–204.

7   Ibid., p. 201

8   Forey, Alan, 'Towards a profile of the Templars', p. 197. The ages are taken at the time of first interrogation, not the time of arrest. The dates are 1307, 1310 and 1310–11. There is no adjustment for the number of Templars who died between the time of arrest and the time of interrogation. Because an adjustment to account for the additional 3.5 years for the later interrogations reduced the number of Templars in the applicable age categories, and to make allowance for the Templars who died after arrest and before interrogation, the basic number of 354 Templar Knights was left unchanged, and all ages and YOS are treated as if they occurred in 1307. This also applies to YOS. The fact of Templar deaths before interrogation/trial is shown in Lord, Evelyn, *The Knights Templar in Britain*, Pearson Education Limited (Edinburgh, 2002), pp. 60, 64, 79.

9   Perkins, Clarence, 'The Knights Templar in the British Isles', *The English Historical Review*, Vol. 25, No. 98 (April 1910), p. 222.

10   Lord, *The Knights Templar in Britain*, p. 194.

11   Ibid.

12   Ibid., pp. 60, 64, 79.

13   Baigent & Leigh, *The Temple and the Lodge*, Arcade Publishing (New York, 1989), p. 66.

14   Addison, Charles, *The History of the Knights Templar* (originally published in London, 1842), Adventure Unlimited Press (Kempton, 2001), p. 213.

15   Baigent & Leigh, *The Temple and the Lodge*, pp. 61–61.

16   Lord, *The Knights Templar in Britain*, p. 192.

BIBLIOGRAPHY

PRIMARY SOURCES

Bernard of Clairvaux, 'In Praise of the New Knighthood, *Liber ad milites Templi: De laude novae militae*', translated by Lisa Coffin, in Wasserman, James, *The Templars and the Assassins.*

Charter by Brother Thomas de Lendesay, Master of the Hospital of St John of Jerusalem, to Robert, Son of Alexander Symple of Hauderstoun, 1354. Translation *Scottish Historical Review*, Vol. 5, pp. 17–21 (1908).

Information, *Ross of Auchlossin against the Possessors of Temple-Lands*, Edinburgh (1706) National Library of Scotland.

National Archives of Scotland, Document No. GD119/34.

National Archives of Scotland, Document No. GD119/35.

National Archives of Scotland, Document No. GD1/1020.

'Templaria', Edinburgh, 1825, reproduced in Burnes, James, *Sketch of the History of the Knights Templar*, Wm. Blackwood & Sons (Edinburgh, 1840).

Upton-Ward, J.M., *The Rule of the Templars*, The Boydell Press (Suffolk, 1992).

SECONDARY SOURCES

Addison, Charles, *The History of the Knights Templar* (originally published in London, 1842), Adventure Unlimited Press (Kempton, 2001).

Baigent, Michael and Leigh, Richard, *The Temple and the Lodge*, Arcade Publishing (New York, 1989).

Baigent, Michael, Leigh, Richard & Lincoln, Henry, *The Holy Blood and the Holy Grail*, Delacorte Press (New York, 1982).

Baker, Nina Brown, *Robert Bruce: King of Scots*, Vanguard Press (New York, 1948).

Barber, Malcolm, 'Supplying the Crusader States', Kedar, B.Z. ed. *The Horns of Hattin* (Jerusalem: Yad Izhak Ben-Zvi; Aldershot: Ashgate Variorum, 1992).

——— ed. *The Military Orders, Fighting for the Faith and Caring for the Sick*, Variorum (Aldershot, 1994).

——— *The New Knighthood, a History of the Order of the Temple*, Cambridge University Press, Canto edition (New York, 1994).

——— *The Trial of the Templars*, Cambridge University Press, Canto edition (Cambridge, 1993).

Barbour, Master John, *The Brus*, compiled 1375, translated by George Eyre-Todd, Gowans & Gray Limited (Glasgow, 1907).

Barrow, G.W.S., *Robert Bruce*, University of California Press (Berkeley & Los Angeles, 1965).

Brown, Dan, *The Da Vinci Code*, Doubleday (New York, 2003).

Burman, Edward, *The Templars, Knights of God*, Destiny Books (Rochester, 1986).

Burnes, James, *Sketch of the History of the Knights Templar*, Wm. Blackwood & Sons (Edinburgh, 1840).

Butler, Alan and Dafoe, Stephen, *The Warriors and the Bankers, a History of the Knights Templar From 1307 to the Present*, Templar Books (Ontario, Canada, 1998).

Butler, Alan & Ritchie, John, *Rosslyn Revealed, A Library in Stone*, O Books (Winchester, 2006).

Cooper, Robert L.D., *The Rosslyn Hoax? Viewing Rosslyn Chapel from a new perspective*, Lewis (UK, 2006).

Coppens, Philip, *The Stone Puzzle of Rosslyn Chapel*, Frontier Publishing (the Netherlands, 2004).

Cowan, Ian B., Mackay, P.H.R. & Macquarrie, Alan, *The Knights of St. John of Jerusalem In Scotland*, Scottish History Society, Clark constable Ltd. (Edinburgh, 1983).

Dalrymple, Sir David, *Annals of Scotland*, William Creech (Edinburgh, 1797).

Edwards, John, 'The Knights Templar in Scotland', *Transactions of the Scottish Ecclesiological Society*, Vol. IV (Aberdeen, 1912–1915).

Fawtier, Robert, *The Capetian Kings of France, Monarch & Nation (987–1328)*, Macmillan/St Martins Press (London, 1960).

Forey, Alan, 'Towards a Profile of the Templars in the Early Fourteenth Century', Barber, Malcolm, ed. *The Military Orders, Fighting for the Faith and Caring for the Sick*, Variorum (Aldershot, 1994).

Frale, Barbara, *The Knights Templar, The Secret History Revealed*, Arcade Publishing (New York, 2009).

Gardner, Lawrence, *Bloodline of the Holy Grail*, Barnes & Noble (New York, 1997).

Gerber, Pat, *Stone of Destiny*, Conongate Books Ltd (Edinburgh, 1997).

Haag, Michael, *The Templars, the History and the Myth*, Harper Collins (New York, 2009).

Hallam, Elizabeth, ed. *Chronicles of the Crusades*, CLB International (Surrey, 1989).

Hallam, Elizabeth, *The Plantagenet Chronicles*, CLB Publishing, Crescent Books (Surrey, 1995).

Howarth, Stephen, *The Knights Templar*, Barnes & Noble (New York, 1992).

Knight & Lomas, *The Second Messiah*, Element (1997).

Laidler, Keith, *The Head of God, The Lost Treasure of the Templars*, Orion edn (1999).

Lane, Alan & Campbell, Ewan, *Dunadd, An Early Dalriadic Capital*, Oxbow Books (Oxford, 2000).

Leighton, John M., *History of the County of Fife*, vol. 3, Joseph Swan (1840).

Linkbater, Eric, *The Survival of Scotland*, Doubleday & Co. (New York, 1968).

Lord, Evelyn, *The Knights Templar in Britain*, Pearson Education Limited (Edinburgh, 2002).

MacQuarrie, Alan, *Scotland and the Crusades, 1095–1560*, John Donald Publishers, Ltd (Edinburgh, 1985).

Magnusson, Magnus, *Scotland: The Story of a Nation*, Atlantic Monthly Press (New York, 2000).

Maidment, James, ed. *Abstract of the Charters and other papers recorded in the Chartulary of Torphichen from 1581 to 1596* (Edinburgh, 1830).

Mann, William F., *The Labyrinth of the Grail*, Laughing Owl Publishing, Inc. (Grand Bay, 1999). Also published under the title *Knights Templar in the New World*, Destiny Books, Rochester, Vermont.

Markale, Jean, *The Templar Treasure at Gisors*, Inner Traditions (Rochester, 2003).

Maxwell, Sir Herbert, Bart. M.P., *Robert the Bruce and the Struggle for Scottish Independence*, 2nd edn, G.P. Putnam & Son, The Knickerbocker Press (New York, 1897).

Michael, Prince of Albany, *The Forgotten Monarchy of Scotland*, Element (Shaftesbury, Dorset, 1998).

Nicholson, Helen, *Templars, Hospitallers and Teutonic Knights, Images of the Military Orders, 1128–1291*, Leicester University Press (London, 1995).

——— *The Knights Templar, A New History*, Sutton Publishing Ltd (Gloucestershire, 2001).

Olsen, Oddvar, *The Templar Papers*, New Page Books (Franklin Lakes, 2006).

Parker, Thomas, *The Knights Templars in England*, University of Arizona Press (Tucson, 1963).

Partner, Peter, *The Knights Templar and their Myth*, Destiny Books (Rochester, 1990).

Picket, Lynn & Prince, Cliff, *The Templar Revelation*, Touchstone, Simon & Schuster (New York, 1998).

Proceedings of the Society of Antiquaries of Scotland, 'Temple Midlothian', vol. XLVI, (Edinburgh, 1911–1912).

Ralls, Karen, *Knights Templar Encyclopedia*, New Page Books (Franklin Lakes, 2007).

———— *The Templars and the Grail*, Quest Books (Wheaton, 2003).

Read, Piers Paul, *The Templars*, St Martins Press (New York, 1999).

Robinson, John J., *Born in Blood, the Lost Secrets of Freemasonry*, M. Evens & Co. (New York, 1989).

Runciman, Steven, *The History of the Crusades*, vol. 3, Cambridge University Press (London, 1954).

Sadler, John, *Scottish Battles, From Mons Graupious to Culloden*, Canongate Books, Ltd (Edinburgh, 1996).

Sanello, Frank, *The Knights Templar, God's Warriors, the Devil's Bankers*, Taylor Trade Publishing, (Lanham, 2003).

Scott, Ronald McNair, *Robert the Bruce, King of Scots*, Carroll & Graf Publishers (New York, 1996).

Shonfield, Hugh, *The Essene Oddessey*, Element (Shaftesbury, 1993).

Simon, Edith, *The Piebald Standard, A Biography of the Knights Templar*, Little, Brown & Co. (Boston, 1959).

Sinclair, Andrew, *Rosslyn, The Story of Rosslyn Chapel and the True Story Behind the Da Vinci Code*, Birlinn Limited (Edinburgh, 2006).

———— *The Sword and the Grail*, Birlinn Limited (Edinburgh, 2002).

Sora, Steven, *The Lost Treasure of the Knights Templar*, Destiny Books (Rochester, 1999).

Statutes of the Religious and Military Order of The Temple, as Established in Scotland with An Historical Notice of the Order, 'Historical Notice of the Order', 1843, 2nd edn, Alex, Laurie and Co. (Edinburgh, 1964).

Thys, Leo, *History of The Order of the Temple of Jerusalem*, Stewart Graphic (East Kilbride, 2005).

Turnbull, Michael T.R.B., *Rosslyn Chapel Revealed*, Sutton Publishing (Gloucestershire, 2007).

Wallace-Murphy, Tim & Hopkins, Marilyn, *Rosslyn, Guardian of the Secrets of the Holy Grail*, Element (Shaftesbury, 1999).

Watson, Fiona & Anderson, Maggi, *The Battle of Bannockburn*, a Report for Stirling Council (Viewforth, Stirling, May 2001).

Wormald, Jenny, ed. *Scotland: A History*, Oxford University Press (Oxford, 2005).

Wasserman, James, *The Templars and the Assassins: The Militia of Heaven*, Inner Traditions, Destiny Books (Rochester, 2001).

Way of Plean, George & Squire, Romilly, *Scottish Clan & Family Encyclopedia*, HarperCollins (Glasgow, 1994).

ARTICLES

Aitken, Robert, 'The Knights Templars in Scotland', *The Scottish Review* (July 1898).

Edwards, John, 'The Templars in Scotland in the Thirteenth Century', *The Scottish Historical Review*, Vol. 5 (1908).

McKerracher, Archie, 'Bruce's Secret Weapon', *The Scots Magazine* (June 1991).

———— 'Who Won at Bannockburn?' *The Highlander* (July/August 1994).

Pearse, Bowen, 'Were the Knights Templar at the Battle at Bannockburn?' *The Highlander* (May/June 2008).

Perkins, Clarence, 'The Trial of the Knights Templar in England', *The English Historical Review*, Vol. 24, No. 95 (July 1909).

———— 'The Knights Templar in the British Isles', *The English Historical Review*, Vol. 25, No. 98 (April 1910).

Robinson, Lin, 'The Knights Templar at Bannockburn – A Rebuttal', *The Highlander* (September/October 2008).

Walker, Alexander, 'The Knights Templars In & Around Aberdeen', *The Aberdeen Journal*, Aberdeen University Press (16 March 1887).

Worden, Ian P., *The Round Church of Ophir, Orkney*, Occasional Paper No. 6, Institute of Geomantic Research (Cambridge, 1976).

'Templar Notes', *The Scottish Knights Templar*, published by the Stirling Commandery (January 1987).

'Soirée of the White Cockade', *The Scottish Knights Templar*, published by the Stirling Commandery (1986–87).

PRIVATE PUBLICATION

Coutts, Rev. Alfred, *The Knights Templar in Scotland* (Edinburgh, 1890).

Sherry de Achaea, Francis Andrew, GCOT, Grand Prior of Scotland, 'The Templar', undated.

Standing, Howard, *The Scottish Knights Templar, Outremer* (1995).

WEBSITES

Autonomous Grand Priory of Scotland, www.skt.org.uk

Grand Priory of the Knights Templar in Scotland, www.scottishknight-stemplar.org

Ordo Supremus Militaris Templi Hierosolymitani (OSMTH International), www.osmth.org

Rosslyn Chapel, www.rosslynchapel.com

Rosslyn Templars, www.rosslyntemplars.org.uk

The Grand Priory of Scotland, www.scottishtemplarknights.info

TELEVISION

'In Search of History™ The Knights Templar,' © 1997 A & E Television Networks.

OTHER

SMOTJ, Inc. *v.* de Sousa Fontes, case No. U.S.D.C. Tex. No. 3-995CV-0890Gß

INDEX

Abbey of Maubuisson 89
Abbey of Newbattle 48
Abbey of Scone 80
Aberdeen 40, 61, 67, 99, 117, 159
Aberdeen Philosophical Society
    64
Aberdeenshire 66, 183
Aboyne, valley of 40, 66, 71
Acre 24, 36, 94, 171–3
    fall of 28, 33, 94, 102
    Frederick II arrival 34
    impact of losses 84, 98
    location 37
    new headquaters 32, 37
Addison, Charles C. 175
Ad providam 39, 141
Agnus Dei (Lamb of God) 134
Akiney, Roger de 53
Alamut – the Eagle's Nest 31
Alexander II, King of Scotland
    50, 71
Alexander IV, Pope 66
al-Kamil, Sultan 34

Amalric 30–1
Anacletus II of Rome 28
Antioch 29
Apprentice Pillar 133–4
Aquitaine, Eleanor of 29, 98
Arbroath Abbey 61
D'Argentan, Sir Giles 170
Argyle 40, 63, 101, 160
    evidence of Templar presence
      99
    Templar landing in 100
    Templars sailed to 93
Ark of the Covenant 17, 132–3
Artois, Count Robert of 35
Assassins 30–1
Atlit 29, 33, 37
Autonomous Grand Priory of
    Scotland 69, 156, 161
Ayer, town of 99
Ayrshire 66–7

Baigent, Michael 17, 90, 99–100,
    174–5

baillies 23, 109, 140–2
baillis 24, 55, 63, 65, 70
Balantrodoch
  business at 50
  general purpose 46, 50
  hierarchy 50
  lifestyle 50–1
  Masters 53
  origin of name 48
  Preceptory boundaries 49
  Latin inscription 56
  transfer to Hospitallers 56
  Temple, final days 56–7
Baldwin I of Jerusalem 16
Balgonie Castle 67, 69, 161
Balliol, John 76–7
Baphomet 136
Barber, Malcolm 19, 40, 88
Barbour, John 119, 143
Bartholomew, Master of
      Balantrodoch 53
Battle of
  Culloden 149
  Hattin 28, 31–2, 37
  Killiecrankie 147–8
  Mansurah 35
  Stirling Bridge 65
Beauseant 22
Belfast Lough 99
Binning, John 144
Bisol, Godfrey 16
Boulogne, Peter de 97, 100
Brydon, Robert 17, 161
Burnes, James 56
Byset, Walter 61, 66

Capet, Hugh 86
Carey, Rear Admiral James J. 157

Carrickfergus 99
Castle at Destriot 29, 33
Castle Sween 99, 101
Châlons, Hugh de 84, 88, 95, 97
Chalon, Jean de 96
Champagne, Count de 16
Chappes, Elisabeth de 47, 100
Charney, Geoffroi de 39, 89
Charter of Larmenius 155
Chartres Cathedral 136
Chinon Castle 39, 109, 111
Chinon Parchment 39
Church of Scotland 101, 104
Church of the Holy Sepulcher 49
Cistercian monks 19, 49
Cistercian Abbey 48–9
Clairvaux, Bernard de 18–19, 24,
      26–8, 48
Clement V, Pope 11, 39, 81, 84, 90,
      97, 101
  Council of Vienna 39
  dissolves the Templars 17, 25,
      47, 60, 69, 157
  hearings at Chinon 39
  Inquisition 12, 89, 97
  excommunication of Bruce 81
  Templar arrests in England 107
  Templar arrests in France 89, 95
  transfers Templar Property to
      Hospitallers 141, 144
Clifton, Walter de 53, 165
  death of 112
  flight of other Templars 108
  Inquisition 108–10, 112, 117,
      122
  Preceptor of Scotland 140
Commander (Master) of the City
      of Jerusalem 22

Commandery of Jacques de
    Molay 161
Commandery of Nova Scotia 164
Compline 19, 50
Comrie, Gordon McGregor 162
Comyn, John 'The Red' 76–80,
    102, 170
Comyn, John, Earl of Buchan 103,
    116
Conyers, Hugh de 53
Cook, Richard 55
Cooper, Robert L.D. 171
Corbet, Ranulph de 53
Council of Pisa 28
Council of Troyes 24, 26–8, 48, 84
Council of Vienna 39, 60
Courtrai, Templar defeat at 86, 94
Coutts, Alfred 112
Culter, town of 40
Crusades 30, 50, 84, 86, 88
    first 16
    second 29
    third 32
    fourth 32
    fifth 32–3
    sixth 33
    seventh 35, 54
    Children's Crusade 32
    and Bruce 170
Cyprus 32, 41, 50
    last Templar stronghold in the
        East 86
    maintenance of 94

Dail Righ, battle of 103
Damascus 24, 38
David I, King of Scotland 46–8,
    51, 53

John Balliol and 76
*Deo et Sancto Hospitali de Jerusalem
    et fratribus ejusdem Militiae
    Templi Salamonis* 70, 144
Deuchar, Alexander 137, 143,
    149–51, 161
Diniz, King of Portugal 40
Dome on the Rock 34
Douglas, Sir James 103, 118–19
    death of 142
    The Good Sir James 142
    The Black Douglas 112
Dunfermline, town of 67
Dunfermline Abbey 136
Dunstaffnage Castle 117

Edinburgh 23, 46, 67, 71, 81, 129,
    140, 145, 158
    Alexander Deuchar 149
    bailli of 55
    capture by Bruce 118
    Inquisition in 108
    OSMTH meeting 163
Edward I, King of England 54–5,
    76, 84, 101, 108, 170
    Bruce's excommunication 81
    Hammer of the Scots 116
    John Balliol 76
    Stone of Scone/Destiny 160
Edward II, King of England
    Bannockburn 119, 124, 140
    Inquisition 109, 112
    Templar arrests in England 100,
        108
    torture 107
Edward III 143
Esperston, Estate at 54–5, 144
Eugenius III, Pope 29

Falkirk, Battle of 54–5
Falkirk, town of 67
Fergus Mor mac Eirc 160
Fifeshire 67, 72
Firth of Clyde 63, 99, 103, 169
Firth of Forth 69, 100
Firth of Lorne 101
Flanders 78, 99
Florian, Esquiu de 37
Flote, Pierre 84, 91
Frederick II 33–5
    Holy Roman Emperor 34
    King of Germany 33
    treaty with Saracens 34–5

Galileo Galilei 39
Gillies Hill 123–4
Gisors
    town 96
    treasure 104, 105
Glasgow 61, 102, 158, 163
Glen Trool 116–17
Goodwin, Thomas 144
Graham, John of Claverhouse,
    Viscount Dundee 146–8, 162
Grand Priory of Scotland
    1962–1993 157–9
    Present 162–3
Grand Priory of the Knights
    Templar in Scotland 163
Grand Priory of the Scots 164–6
Gregory III, Pope 33
Grey Friars
    Monastery 77, 79–80
    Monks 78

Halidon Hill 143
Hashishiyun 30

Hay, Father Richard Augustine
    130
Heisterback, Caesarius of 52
Henry I, King of England 24, 47–8
Henry III, King of England 63
Henry VIII, King of England 57
Henry, Holy Roman Emperor 170
Holy Grail 17, 47, 132–4
Holyrood
    Abbey 108–11, 117
    Palace 148
    Prince Charles and 149, 158
    testimony at 111, 117
Hopkins, Marilyn 41
Hospitallers 46, 71, 73, 145–6
    Balantrodoch 52
    transfer of Templar properties
        to 39, 69–70, 141–2, 144–5
    transfer of properties to Queen
        Mary 71, 145–6
    Templars, efforts to unit with
        84, 86, 88
    trial over Esperston Estate 56
Huseflete, John de 53–4, 108, 112

Innocent II, Pope 28
Inverness 99, 147, 159
Isabella 50
Isle of Islay 101
Isle of Mey 100
Isle of Ruad 37

Jacobites 146–7, 149
James IV, King of Scotland 70,
    144–5
James V, King of Scotland 70
James VII/II, King of Scotland
    and England 147

James the Just 17
Jay, Brian de 53, 175
   death 55
   Esperston 54–5
   Inquisition 111
Jerusalem 16–56 *passim*
Jesus of Nazareth 17, 21, 133, 135–6
Joinville, Count John de 36
Jura, the Sound of 99, 101

Keith, Sir Robert of 119, 121–2
   calvary, the *coup de grace* 124
Keith, Sir William of Galston 132
Kelso Abbey 61–2
Kilmartin 99, 101
Kilmory 99, 101
Kingcausie, site 40, 67, 70–1
Kinghorn, town of 67, 72
Kintyre Peninsula 101
Kirkliston 64, 66
Kirkpatrick, Roger of 80
   excommunicated 80
Knights of Christ 40, 93
Knollis, Sir William 56
Knollis, William 70

La Roche de Roussel 29
La Rochelle, Port of 29, 93,
   96–100
Lamberton, William, Bishop of St
   Andrews 80–1, 108, 111–12,
   122
Larmenius, Johannes Marcus 155,
   157
Leigh, Richard 41, 90, 99–100,
   174–5
Leighton, Alexander de 144
letters of credit 33, 54

Leuprecht, Baron Anton 157, 162
Lindesay, Thomas de 56
Lindsey, James of 56
Lindsey, Walter 145
Linlithgow, 118
Lisours, William de 144
Lisours, William de, the elder 143
Lochmaben 79
London Temple 50
Lord Acton 26
Loudon Hill 116
Louis IX, King of France 35–6
Louvre, the 86, 94–5

Macdonalds 101
MacDonald, Angus Og 101, 123
MacDougalls 101, 103–4, 117
MacDougall, John of Lorn 103
Mackay, Major General Hugh 147
MacLeod, Dr Ian 136, 170
Maidment, James 66
Malcolm IV, King of Scotland 51,
   54
Mamluks 28, 37
Mandeville, Sir John 85
Marshal 22
Martin, Sir Robert 150
Mary Magdalene 17
Mary, Queen of Scotland 67, 71,
   131, 145
Maryculter, town of 67
Maryculter, Temple at 40, 51–2,
   61–2, 64, 66, 108
   abandoned 62
   Kelso Monk dispute 62
   relation to Balantrodoch 61
   sale of 70–1
Mason's Pillar 133–4

Maxwell, Sir Herbert 79
McGrath, James 159, 162
Mesnil, Walter de 31
Michael, John 26
Middle Ages 18, 21, 48
Middleton, William de 53–4, 108–9
    after the Inquisition 111
Militi Templi Scotia 143, 151, 156,
    159–61, 163
Militia Dei 29
Milne, Admiral Sir David 151
Molay, Jacques de 39, 83, 96, 98,
    155–7
    arrest 89, 95
    becomes Grand Master 85
    curses king and pope 39
    execution of 39
    meeting at Poitiers 86
    orders Templar treasure shipped
        out of France 40, 97
Monthar, Andrew de 16
Montidier, Payens de 16
Morris, Raymond Stanley of
    Balgonie and Eddergoll 68,
    164–5
Mount Carmel 29, 33
Mowbray, Sir Philip 118

Naillac, Philibert de 144
Neave, Dr Richard 125, 136, 170
Newbattle
    Abbey of 48–9
    Abbot of 110
    town of 65
Nogaret, Guillaume de 84, 91

Oban, town of 101
Omne datum optimum 28–9

Order of the Poor Knights of
    Christ and the Temple of
    Solomon 16
*Ordo Supremus Militaris Templi
    Hierosolymitani* (Original) 16
*Ordo Supremus Militaris Templi
    Hierosolymitani* (OSMTH)
    137, 154–8, 160–2
Orkney Islands 41, 100
Ottomans 41
Outremer *passim*
    Atlit and 33, 37
    Children's Crusade and 32–3
    Christian attitude in 34
    definition 16
    Frederick II exit from 35
    Muslim effectiveness in 27–8
    recovery by Richard I 32
    Templars' lifespan in 20
    the end of the European
        presence 37

Pairaud, Hugh de 84, 86, 89, 93,
    95–7
Palestine 15–17, 24, 28–9
Paris Temple 40, 86–7, 93–5, 97
Paris, Guillaume de 89
Pastoralis praeeminentiae 100, 107
Patrick, Earl of Dunbar 54
Payens, Hughes de 16–18, 24, 26,
    28, 46–9, 100, 105, 162
Payens, village of 16
Payns, town of 26
Pembroke, Earl of 116
Perth, City of 117, 147
Peterculter 61–2
Philip IV, King of France (Philip
    le Bel [the Fair]) *passim*

Capetian king 86
currency devaluation and debt
  87–8
Edward II's response to his
  order 107
income sources 87
order for the Templars' arrests
  37
Templars and debt 88
Picquigny, Warmund of 20
Poitiers, town of 86, 97
Port Bonnet 29
Preston, William de 109
Provence, Count of 16

Ralph, Bishop of Aberdeen 66
Randolph, Thomas, Earl of Moray
  118–19
Raymouard 108, 117
Reamhair, Duncan 123
Reformation, the 46, 53, 131,
  144–5
Reformation, Act of 57
Remois, Matthew du, Cardinal-
  Bishop of Albano 26
Richard I (the Lionheart), King of
  England 32, 34
Rideforte, Garad de 32
River Dee 61–2, 66
River Seine 16, 39, 93, 98–9
Robert I, Lord of Annandale
  also Robert the Competitor
  76–7
Robert, Master of Balantrodoch
  53
Robert the Bruce, *passim*
  agreement with John Comyn
  77

confrontation with King
  Edward I 78–9
crowned King of Scotland 80
death mask in Rosslyn Chapel?
  135
excommunication lifted 81
Galloway and Carrick 108
heart to the Holy Land 142
impact of excommunication 81
leadership 125
meeting with John Comyn 79
size of army 119
Robert, Master at Balantrodoch
  53
Roslin, village of 47–8, 129
Ross of Auchlossin 72
Rosslyn Chapel
  location 47, 129
  modern Templars 137, 161, 164
  reformation 131
  Templar treasure 41, 49
Rosslyn Templars 164
Roxburgh Castle on Shrove 118
Ruad, Isle of 35, 85

St Aman, Archambaud de 16, 26
St Amand, Odo de 31
St Andrews, Priory of 63, 67
St Clair, Henry de, Earl of Orkney
  109
St Clair, James 131
St Clair, Sir Oliver 130–1
St Clair, Sir William 100
  Robert the Bruce 103
  buried in Rosslyn Chapel 132
St Clair, Sir William 130, 133
St Clair, William de 109
Saint Clair(s) 47, 49, 132–4, 137

Balantrodoch 49
  Hughes de Payens and 47
  Rosslyn Chapel 49, 130–1
Saint-Claire, Catherine de 47, 49,
  100
St Omer, Godfroi de 16
Saladin, or Sala-ad-Din Yusuf ibn
  Ayyub 28, 30–2
Sandilands, James 131
Sandilands, Sir John 144–6
Saracens 20, 27, 32, 35, 128, 135
Sautre, John de, Master of
  Balantrodoch 53–4
Scott, Sir Walter 143
Scottish Knights Templar 156, 162
Sede, Gerard de 96
Segrave, John de 108
Seneschal 22, 39, 155
Seton, Sir Alexander 121
Seton, David 145–6
Sherry, Francis Andrew 157–8, 162
Sidon, town of 31
Sinclair, Andrew 133–4
Sinclair, William
  gravestone 132
Soirée of the White Cockade 158
Solerio, Master John de 108, 118
Sonne, Guillaume de 35
Sousa Fontes, Antonio Campbell
  Pinto de 155, 157–8, 164–5
Sousa Fontes, Fernando Campbell
  Pinto Pereiro de 155–7,
  161–2
South Esk River 48
Sovereign Military Order of the
  Temple of Jerusalem, Inc.
  156, 164–6
Stella Templum 161, 167

Stewart, George 161
Stewart, HRH Prince Michael
  James of Albany 158
Stirling Castle 118–19, 122, 140,
  160
Stone of Scone/Destiny 159–61
Strathmiglo 67
Stuart, Prince Charles Edward
  'Bonnie Prince Charlie' 148,
  158, 162

Templar Masters in Scotland 53–4
Templar Rule
  chastity 20
  healthcare 25
  obedience 21
  origin 19
  poverty 21
  strict observance 21, 36
Templar, Knights
  arrogance 27, 40, 54, 85, 166
  as monks 25, 27, 103, 111
  avoided capture 173–4
  bankers 24–5
  categories of personnel 23
  charges against 37–8, 110–11
  decline and fall 30–7
  enemy 27–8
  fleet 24
  growth 28–30
  hierarchy 21–2
  history 26–7
  number arrested 89–90
  on the battlefield 20
  origin 16
  properties 66–9
  revenue from Scotland 61, 65
  treasury in Paris 94–5

unification with Hospitallers
    86, 88, 141–2, 144, 146
warriors and entrepreneurs 24
Temple Liston 66, 71
Temple Mount 41, 130
Temple of Solomon 16–17, 34,
    130, 133
Temple, village of 46–8, 57
Terrae Templariae 70, 141
Thame, Brother Philip de 141
Theobaklus, Franciscus 155
Tiberias, City of 31
Torphichen 56, 71, 142, 144–5
Tortosa, City of 37, 85
Totti, Thomas 53, 108
Tyre, William of 29

Urban IV, Pope 61

Valois, Catherine de 98
Vandenberg, Emile Clement
    Joseph Isaac 55
Vespers 19
Vichiers, Renaud de 36
Villaret, Fulk de 86
Villiers, Gerard de 84, 89, 95, 97
Vipont, Adam de 143
Vipont, Sir William 143
Vox in excelso 39, 60, 157

Walker, Sir Patrick 151
Wallace-Murphy, Timothy 41
Wedale, Adam de 109
William I, King of Scotland 51, 61
William, son of Geoffrey of
    Halkerston 50
Wishart, Bishop 80, 102–3

ABOUT THE AUTHOR

Robert Ferguson was invested into the Supreme Military Order of the Temple of Jerusalem, Grand Priory of the Scots, in 1998. He is a Knight Commander, is a member of the Order's Privy Council, and has earned special recognition as the Priory's *Avocat*. He is also an active member of the Clan Ferguson Society of North America, and was a Regional Vice President.

The author is an Adjunct Professor of Astronomy (ret.) at the University of La Verne, California. He has also taught telescope optics at the University of California at Los Angeles and at Irvine. He was a co-founder and is currently a member of the Board of Trustees of the Mount Wilson Institute which oversees the operation of the Mount Wilson Observatories.

The author is an attorney at law and practices in the fields of complex business and land use litigation. He is a graduate of the University of Southern California with an A.B. in Economics and a Juris Doctor. He also studied European economics and literature at the University of Vienna, Austria. Between 1994 and 2002 he taught Evidence and Civil Procedure at the University of La Verne's College of Law.

The author lives in southern California.